The
America
Book of Verse

Edited by

FRANCIS X. TALBOT, S.J.

Literary Editor of *America*

THE AMERICA PRESS
NEW YORK

Cum Permissu Superiorum

PS 591
A5
O3

The *America* Book of Verse

PROLOGUE

More than once when I have been on the trail of an elusive fact hidden somewhere in the earlier numbers of *America,* I have tarried in my quest to cast a glance at a poem which turned up on a chance page. And not once only was I so diverted by the poem that I quite forgot the fact by virtue of the fancy. A princess walked serene through an army of peasants. A diamond glowed in a quarry of granite. A living thought lay smothered in a vault of paper. It came to me that the princess should be rescued from her environment and the diamonds should be set in coronets. The living thought should be given air. The poems deserved a better eternity than that of being found by someone who was searching for something else.

The blame or the credit of inflicting or bestowing a new anthology on the patient or the eager public does not devolve on me alone. I have been urged and dared to do the deed. I have seen these poems quoted, yes and pirated, by many periodicals. I have read them in other anthologies and among the collected poems of the authors. A few days ago, I was startled when I heard an after-dinner speaker conclude his highly emotional address by declaiming an entire poem published in *America* on that very date. Perhaps the editing of this anthology may be pardoned.

Anthologies and books of "best poems" follow the general rule of disappointing me. I have no guarantee that this collection may not likewise leave you cold in your emotions or unchilled in your spine by that thrill that comes occasionally when you first read a startling bit of literature. But I can confess that many of the poems here included have either warmed me or chilled me, and what is more have done so when I read them in manuscript and when I corrected them in proof and when I reread them on the clean, shiny page of the magazine. They will probably stir the embers when my soul inhabits an ancient body. Such a confession, of course, argues nothing for other readers. Anthologists have the privilege as well as the duty of sipping the nectar that pleases them.

This anthology should have been much better than it is. This is said by way of explanation rather than of apology. In the first two volumes of *America* only eleven poems were published and in the succeeding fifteen volumes there was not even one poem. During several more volumes, a very occasional poem was permitted to slip in. It was not until three or four years ago that poetry began to be welcomed rather than tolerated in *America*. Because of the ban against the poets in the earlier volumes of *America,* this anthology has been deprived of some exquisite verse. First, because it might have contained several poems by such masters as Louise Imogen Guiney and Maurice Francis Egan and Joyce Kilmer and others who were inspired in those days. Second, because the literary editors of *America* during those years were James J. Daly, S.J., who is a commanding poet in his own right and a critic of discernment, and Walter Dwight, S.J., whose taste in poetry was a keen and a sure instinct. Editors such as these would have attracted the best of Catholic poetry to *America* and would have tolerated nothing but the best. The poems that might have been published would bulk large in this volume. In a spirit of arrogance I may add that such poems, had they existed, would not have replaced any that are in this anthology. The book would merely have been larger.

This is not a general anthology of current verse. It contains exclusively the poems which have been originally published in the columns of *America*. In its arrangement, it departs from the usual mode of herding all of a poet's fancies together under his name. There may be efficiency and good order in an alphabetical sequence of poets, there may be a scientific precision in heading the procession with Abel and closing it with Zuzu. But the matter and the mood of a poem is of more consequence than is the name of its author. Hence, these verses have been grouped together according to their kinship with one another. A thread links them together, a tenuous thread it may appear at times, and a mystic thread at other times, even a thread that is invisible. But this concerns merely the sequence of the poems. A stronger thread there is that binds them all together like the golden chain that pierces the beads of the Rosary.

FRANCIS X. TALBOT, S.J.

CONTENTS

VESTIGES

TESTAMENTS

[xiii]

HOMAGES

IMAGES

A WOMAN COMMENDS HER LITTLE SON

To the aid of my little son
  I call all the magnalities,
Archangel, Dominion,
  Powers and Principalities,

Mary without a stain,
  Joseph that was her spouse,
All God's women and men
  Out of His glorious House,

The Twelve Apostles by him:
  Matthew and Mark and John,
Luke, the Evangelists, nigh him
  So he fight not alone!

Patrick, Columcille, Bride,
  The Saints of the Irish nation,
Kieran, Kevin, beside
  In the death and the desolation.

Listen, ye Soldier-Saints,
  Sebastian, Ignatius, Joan,
Be by his side; if he faints
  Strengthen my little son.

In the Side of Christ I lay him
  In the Wound that the spear made,
In the pierced Hands I stay him
  So I am not afraid.

3

On the knees of the Blessed Mary,
   And in the fold of her arm,
Refuge and sanctuary
   Where he shall take no harm.

To the Wound in the Heart of Christ,
   To the Trinity Three in One;
To the Blood spilled out, unpriced,
   For love of my little son.

                              KATHARINE TYNAN.

THE BERRY-BLOSSOM

Agnes Lawlor walks alone,
   And they say what she desires
Is as fair as the berry-blossom known
   To be among the briers.

But when she comes to the Chapel-gate,
   I'll have a word or two
With "Agnes, girl, 'tis you'd be late
   If I had walked with you."

And maybe she shall answer me
   With the humor of the heart:
"If I were going to Mass with ye
   'Tis early I would start."

Or maybe she might answer me
   With the humor of the soul:
"And if I were coming from Mass with ye
   The silence would be droll."

For the words of Agnes scarcely could
   Be warmer than they are,
But the fear is on me that she would
   Not travel with me far;

4

Since Agnes Lawlor walks alone
  On her Communion morns,
Bedecked with a Berry-Blossom known
  To have been among the thorns.

FRANCIS CARLIN.

THE RIVALS

And now Veronica Johnson
  Has gone to be a nun,
After all the time I've spent on her
  And all the things I've done.

I courted Veronica Johnson
  And gave her books and flowers,
And I loaned her my new umbrella
  To take her home in showers.

I trimmed the rose-bush at her door;
  I often mowed the grass.
And she had me wearing medals
  And trotting off to Mass.

But when I asked her for her hand
  She never gave a nod;
She threw me down completely
  And went running off with God.

Would you think that one so cruel
  Could ever, ever be—
With her highfalutin' notions
  About eternity!

She said it was her Maker
  Who bade her leave and go.
Good Lord, unless you *make* a girl
  You haven't got a show!

LEONARD FEENEY, S.J.

ELECTUS

Marie proclaimed him precious fool,
    Sweet lark, more lovable than wise—
But once she caught a glimpse of tall
    Lit candles in his eyes;

She feared such flames of mystery
    And blew at them her beauty's breath;
And never knew why sun and stars
    Must throb and burn to death.

And when he went the odd, white way
    That skims the lakes of Paradise—
Marie searched well each lover's look
    For candles in his eyes.

             THOMAS BUTLER FEENEY, S.J.

WEE MARY'S PASSING

The other evening, down in Knock
    And just about to cross the rill,
I met a man from Carrickshock
    Whose little one had long been ill.

"And how is she?" said I to Tim;
    Not knowing as he crossed the ford
That the sally-rod he had with him
    Was measure for a coffin-board.

"And how is who?" said Tim to me,
    "Wee Mary, Heaven be good to her,
Was the only one I had and she
    Is ready for the carpenter."

"Och, man!" said I, "and is it so?
    God's comfort to ye in her death!"
The while a memory whispered low:
    "The Carpenter of Nazareth."

             FRANCIS CARLIN.

ARTISTRY

Of what strange matter has God made the girl—
Elusive as the dews that shaggy hedges pearl
Before they melt within the kisses of the sun.
She is a golden dream but half begun,
A fairy leading through alluring ways,
With all the fragrant morning in her gaze.
She is the laughter of all noon-day skies,
The sudden mist of tears in evening's faded eyes.
She is a sigh from passing sadness sprung,
A song of life with all its lines unsung.
She is the mother of a race to be,
The moulder of a nation's destiny.
She is a white seed prisoned in a stirring clod,
Spirit and earth—what whimsy in the mind of God
To make the girl and let her young hands hold
All flowers of love and life as they unfold.

SISTER M. ELEANORE, C.S.C.

LEARNING

How shall I thank Him who reveals to me
   The depths of your soul that He has made
So intimately His, wherein I see
   His image which is always there displayed?
How shall I thank Him that He stooped to kiss
   My sleeping heart and, very gently, said:
"Awake, O foolish heart! Behold your bliss!
   Awake and love, for beauty is not dead!"
How shall I thank Him when I stand, at last,
   Dazzled by trembling clouds of Seraphim—
There where there is no future and no past,
   But an exquisite present, lost in Him?
Perhaps, by gazing often on your face
   I shall learn how to thank Him for this grace.

MARY DIXON THAYER.

FAVORITES

"Now which is your favorite doll?" I asked
   Of little Jane Marie.
"My old rag doll without any arms
   I love the best," said she.

"And which of these kittens that play about
   Is the one that you love best?"
"Oh the poor little thing without any tail
   I love above the rest."

"And of all the boys I know at school
   The one that I prefer—
Is you!" she cried; and she ran away
   Before I could answer her.

And I looked at the blear-eyed cat she chose
   And the doll in faded pink;
And I ran to the mirror and looked at me—
   And I tell you it made me think.

               THOMAS BUTLER FEENEY, S.J.

THE SECRET

One night when little Eileen put
   The buttermilk to cool
All in a wee, black pail—she looked
   And saw with great surprise
A thousand stars and a silver moon
   Reflected in the pool,
In the bucket of fresh-churned buttermilk
   Left out beneath the skies.

Now Eileen then was young in ways,
   And wonder made her think
No show of beauty as fair as this
   Could ever again befall;

Then a fit of passion seized her
    And with one unbroken drink
She drained the wee pail of buttermilk,
    The moon, the stars and all!

The good folk thought the little girl
    Would never the least amount
To such a child of beauty that
    She is—to all surprise.
But did they know what I've told to you,
    I think it would account
For the strange, sweet look of starlight
    Ever beaming in her eyes.

THOMAS BUTLER FEENEY, S.J.

THE BLIND GIRL

Would God that I could run and play
Across His fields of wheat,
And dally in the sunshine
That warms His children's feet;
And walk among His flowers
And watch their hungry mouths
Thankfully taste His raindrops
And droop their heads and drowse.

Yet, Lord, I seem not able
To see Thy mirrorings,
Vision Thy worlds I cannot
Nor any human things;
And light seems always darkness
And in this darkness I
Must grope and wander vainly
In the shadow of a sigh.

But if I seem not able
To see these human things,
Then, Lord, I'm only closer
To Thy finer mirrorings;

And if I miss the sunset
And quiet stars at night,
I see the lights of Heaven
With all my inner sight.

And, Lord, if I were able
To watch the ships at sea
And gaze on lovely ladies
In a manner humanly,
I'd soon forget the whisper
Of an angel that is mine,
And substitute their beauty
For the glory that is Thine!

WILLIAM BERRY.

THE WAY OF THE CROSS

Along the dark aisles
   Of a chapel dim,
The little lame girl
   Drags her withered limb.

And all alone she searches
   The shadows on the walls,
To find the three pictures
   Where Jesus falls.

LEONARD FEENEY, S.J.

TO ELIZABETH

This I have read in some old book and wise,
   Penned long ago by one who understood
The heart of man, and looked with seeing eyes
   Upon the world, and evil things and good:
"Here where all changes and naught can endure,"
   He wrote, "here where all beauty dwells with pain,
And love which at the first was deep and pure
   By love of self is often rendered vain—

10

Here, when the many meet, they meet to turn
  Back from the steep and toilsome upward way;
Few meet to rise together—few, to spurn
  That which is base, to work, and climb, and pray.
Precious is friendship when friend calls to friend,
  'Be strong! Here is my hand. Let us ascend!'"

MARY DIXON THAYER.

PORTRAIT

Her moods remember quiet ways
  From out the stately past;
A dignity and courtesy
  Our age has overcast.

Reverence dwells within her heart,
  Candor in her mind,
And hers are steady lifted eyes
  Not even light can blind.

MUNA LEE.

ON WINGS OF SONG

The light words dropped to silence on my tongue
And I again was loving, gay and young;
And I forgot the knowledge that is life,
The body's toiling and the spirit's strife—
Sweet tears my burning eyelids bathed, the scars
My swelling heart pressed on its prison bars
Were eased of their long agony and cooled,
And I once more remembered that God ruled;
Such blessed pangs of yearning pierced me through,
The sound of voices, glint of morning dew,
The spicy odors that new buds exhale,
The gleam of sods upturned adown the vale,
The breath of flowers floating in the air,
Mist-shrouded faces hovering here and there
Like shreds of things we dream about the dead
That stay and haunt us when the dream has fled;

Down youth and hope and beauty's pleasant lane
I went, enraptured with that spheral strain,
Yea, and dear friends went with me, who are dead,
And long have lain with stone at feet and head;
The dun clouds parted on our sky's soft blue,
Those blue deeps opened and our souls went through—
When she sang!

Margaret H. Lawless.

WHEN SHEILA SITS BEFORE HER HARP

When Sheila sits before her harp
   Her fingers touch the sleeping strings,
Like milk-white butterflies that move
   Among green vines on fragile wings.

When Sheila sits before her harp
   And wakes the strains of other days,
I hear the ring of far-fought fields;
   The echo of old hero lays.

When Sheila sits before her harp,
   I see the gaol gates, gaunt and grim,
Rise up to hide the hero's death;
   I hear the *caoine* raised for him.

When Sheila sits before her harp,
   The Sidhe come trooping from their rath;
The King of Ireland's son rides by,
   And hawthorn blooms above his path.

When Sheila rises from her harp,
   And lifts her fingers from the strings,
I see 'twas but a slender girl
   Whose music gave my spirit wings!

Marie Antoinette de Roulet.

HOUR OF TRIUMPH

I

We have, together, mounted the winding road
Up from our childhood's fairyland of dream;
Hand in hand we leaped through compliant gleam
Of a midday sun, and only our dancing slowed
When peaks of disaster and caverns of shade forebode
A waver of path through night by a troubled stream;
Yet, still together, we climbed to the height supreme,
Faint with old years but younger for sharing that load.

Younger, but never again to find fairy field,
Nor shout to far stars with lusty buoyance of youth;
Younger, but alien to young love forever—
Glories lost on the way, from our sight concealed.
Blest is the balm of years, but bitter the truth
That we can turn back . . . . never, and never, and never.

II

Even so, peace. Our age no more admires
With terrible earnestness the things we sought;
By trifles our mind no longer is distraught,
Nor every transient fad our need acquires.
Spent is that red delirium of fires,
Of love and hate with complications fraught,
And we from the mingled joy and pain have brought
Only its love and nothing of its desires.

Never to feel the rush of blood like sap
Course through our veins, and never again to know
Madness of youth, these bitters we are given.
But we have known it all, and now mayhap
On greatest of our adventures we shall go
Peacefully to a port the young call Heaven.

Benjamin Musser.

13

PORTRAIT OF AN OLD LADY

Early one morning as I went a-walking
  I met an old lady so stately and tall,
The red of her cheeks gave a quiver of pleasure
  Like the sight of red hollyhocks by a gray wall.

Fragrance of lavender clung to her, telling
  Of linen piled high on immaculate shelves.
You could fancy her tending her garden or strolling
  Among the proud roses that grow by themselves.

When I am sorrowful, dreading the future,
  Thinking of days when my hair will be gray,
It cheers me to think of that lovely old lady,
  Lavender-haunted and hollyhock-gay.

ALINE KILMER.

THE OLD WOMAN

"I hear the graveyard trees in my head,"
  Said the old, sad woman.
  A little brown leaf, wrinkled and dead
  She seemed, and scarce human,
  Awaiting death's dole.

"I hear in my head the dark, heavy trees,
  Their colloguin' an' sighin';
  Soon," she said "I'll be takin' my ease
  Where my dead are lyin',
  God rest each soul."

CATHAL O'BYRNE.

ON AN OLD WOMAN WHO HAS KNOWN SORROW

She is a gray, immobile, granite tower,
  That the winds cannot move, nor the rains, nor insistent snows;
In the storm-clutched forest of life, where the old trees cower,
  Rooted in rock, each day her life-stream slows.

14

With flint and iron as sap from her withering soul,
  She petrifies to a pattern cold and stern.
What blossoming words could leap from a frozen scroll?
  Though flint may spark on iron, stone cannot burn.

The proudest rivers of earth run deepest-deep—
  Through her, so still, great floods of memory flow;
But a heart of moulding granite cannot weep,
And ears, stone-deaf, men say, know soundest sleep—
  'Tis better so.
                                    J. CORSON MILLER.

AN OLD LADY SINGS

Into a rose-lamp store I goes
  A fine rose-lamp to buy,
For we have a room that looks to the east
  My blind old man and I.

And though we have plenty of dawnings there
  For me to talk about,
It's sunsets folks has need of more
  When youth has flickered out.

So into a rose-lamp store I goes,
  In my mind a wistful plan—
For I'll bring a wee sunset under my arm
  Back home to my blind old man.
                          THOMAS BUTLER FEENEY, S.J.

AFTERTHOUGHTS

'Tis not her goodness, high and white,
That I recall when silent night
Leaves me alone with other days;
Nor her fond care of me,
A child upon her knee;
But all her dear and wilful ways,
Her laugh so gay, her smile so bright:
'Tis these that break my heart at night.
                              FLORENCE GILMORE.

15

THE UNFORGOTTEN

Into the desolate waste that was her youth,
  One love came swiftly, swiftly passed from sight,
Like blossom on a tree whose bleak boughs bore
  Only one April's space their airy white.

Dreary before and after were all her days,
  So that men pitied her whose dream was fleet—
Yet all her life was the richer for those boughs:
  They bore no fruit, but how their bloom was sweet!

MUNA LEE.

MOONLIT FIELDS

Bright carpeting the moon looms yield
  To clothe with mysticism the night;
Long shadows lie across the field
  Like inky stripes on jeweled white.

The shadows waver, moonbeams dance,
  And grasses whisper, strangely stirred;
I turn with quickened, eager glance,
  Thinking it was her voice I heard.

GEORGE LAWRENCE ANDREWS.

MONOTONE

Her lips quivered with gray laughter
  And gray light shuddered in her eyes.
One thought of fog creeping after
  Great slow ships under gray skies.

Death made but little of her dying;
  No more than a young wind at sea
Rewinding a bolt of fog and crying
  An old song in a minor key.

C. T. LANHAM.

LOVE'S YOUNG DREAM

Did you recall, Methuselah,
  When you were white and old,
A maid, a moonlit night and a
  Sweet vow you told?

Methuselah, did you recall
  The song your heart had sung,
When she was fair, and love was all
  And you were young?

And count each lonely century
  And live the days again,
When you were a hundred and twenty and she
  A hundred and ten?

LEONARD FEENEY, S.J.

I DO NOT UNDERSTAND

To still this ageless requiem of pain?
How foolish is the question! You forget,
My dear, death's grayer loneliness, and yet
That loneliness for you is not in vain.
And now green-golden days have come again;
Your presence lingers here where once we met,
Your whispered wind-words breathe a slow regret
That beats through quiet darkness of the rain.

The wings of winds are purple in the night,
And I am quieter now you are gone. . . . .
I cannot bear yet, gleam of cool starlight
Nor half-remembered cadences of song;
Only the clear, white pain of you,—ah, why,
Why, oh my dear, should you have had to die?

ELEANORE L. PERRY.

A WIND ROSE IN THE NIGHT

A wind rose in the night,
  (She had always feared it so!)
Sorrow plucked at my heart
  And I could not help but go.

Softly I went and stood
  By her door at the end of the hall.
Dazed with grief I watched
  The candles flaring and tall.

The wind was wailing aloud:
  I thought how she would have cried
For my warm familiar arms
  And the sense of me by her side.

The candles flickered and leapt,
  The shadows jumped on the wall.
She lay before me small and still
  And did not care at all.

                              ALINE KILMER.

WHERE INNOCENCE LIES SLEEPING

Let us lean across her bed—
You, fulfilled in her, and I who bore—
    Look once more
Alone, upon that wide-browed head, dark-haired head,
    Once rounded cheeks, now thin,
Just parting lips—as if they would begin
Anew to call our names—and while we can,
Praise God together for her little span
    Of life.
Where Innocence lies sleeping
There is no place for weeping:
    So strife
Of grief let us put off awhile,

18

And you at me, and I at you, will smile,
    Before we put away
This little alabaster shell,—
    Tomorrow,
      Shall we not say?—
We on whom there never fell
    Least sorrow
From all her too-short years of care—
Oh Sorrow! what a lovely face you wear!

FLORENCE CHAMPREUX MAGEE.

NIGHT NOISES

Angela died today and went to Heaven;
We counted her summers up and they were seven.
    But why does that trouble you, unloosened shutter,
    That flap at my window in the wind's wild flutter!

Angela's eyes tonight are cold and dim,
Off in the land of song and Seraphim.
    But what does that mean to you, O creaking stair,
    And mice in the wall that gnaw the plaster there!

Angela's little hands are folded white,
Deep in the meadow, under the starry night.
    But why should an ugly gnat keep finely whining
    Around the candle-flame beside me shining!

And never again—and never again will she
Come running across the field to welcome me.
    But, little sheep-bells out on the distant hill,
    Why, at this hour, do you wake and tinkle still!

And not any more—alas!—and not any more,
Will she climb the stairs and knock at my lonely door.
    But, moaning owl in the hayloft overhead,
    How did you come to know that she was dead!

LEONARD FEENEY, S.J.

MIRACLE

Ah strange, that you who loved life's every phase;
Who watched each leaf and fragile bud unfold,
And joyed each pallid snow-drop to behold,
Unseeing, sleep beneath the Easter sprays.
Ah strange, that you, who heard glad songsters raise
Full-throated songs upon a waking wold,
And solved the magic of their liquid gold,
Unmindful lie, throughout their hymns of praise.

Strange, too, that I, who stumble on life's road
With earth-bound feet, and sorrow-blinded eyes,
Should fail to see new grass upreaching there
Above your grave, and only feel the goad
Of pain! No soul of beauty ever dies,
But lives unchanged in realms celestial fair.

LOUISE CRENSHAW RAY.

TIDINGS

Ay . . . they've brought word of him
    From where the poor lad lies,
But all they say, 'tis naught to me
Save only the few words caught for me
    Just when they closed his eyes.

They, with their big brave talk!
    (I'll not hear Brian again).
And how they glorify his deed—
Such babblement, while I that plead
    For tears must wait in vain.

Oh, I'll steal to the green fields,
    And say the words out loud
Somewhere alone, in God's own hush,
And maybe then the tears will gush:
    Not now can *I* be proud.

P. J. O'CONNOR DUFFY.

WHITE LILIES GROW THERE NOW

White as the Hands of Christ, the lilies grow there now
   Where you are lying, dear, where you are sleeping
Beneath the tall slim grasses shadowing your brow,
   Shielding your tired eyes from bitter weeping.
Red poppies grew there once, red as the blood that knew
   The deepest secret of your heart's dear keeping;
But lilies now, for poppies once that wind-like grew
   Have followed through the silent rushes, creeping
Into the deep day's unremembering fold.

White as the Hands of Christ, the lilies grow there now,
   With petal fingers stretched to Heaven, praying
As I have known you pray with quiet voice and low,
   In deep communion with the Virgin, saying,
"Ave Maria . . . gratia plena . . . amen."
   Unworldly lady, Heaven is displaying
A whiter star tonight for now you live again;
   While lilies that I know are slightly swaying
On slender stems deep-rooted in your soul.

NORBERT ENGELS.

THE CARDINAL'S GARDEN

Though I am young, when old folks whisper,
   "For years the Cardinal has been dead!"
They stare at me in startled wonder,
   Because I listen and shake my head,
Because I turn from them with laughter,
   Never heeding what they have said.

Though I am foolish, when wise fools tell me,
   "The Cardinal sleeps in his narrow tomb!"
I turn away from their mournful voices,
   Breathing of death and the grave's dark doom,
For I have leaned through the twilight shadows
   To watch the Cardinal's garden bloom.

Though I am young, when folks are saying,
  "No more the Cardinal heeds our tears!"
They stare at me, while I am mocking
  Their empty doubts and their futile fears,
For I have walked in the Cardinal's garden,
  When spring came flouting the long-dead years.

Though I am foolish, when wise folk whisper,
  "Long has the Cardinal dwelled afar!"
I turn from them with a heart of pity,
  Because they are blind to the things that are,
For I have walked in his lilac garden
  With the Cardinal and a ghostly star.

EDGAR DANIEL KRAMER.

A REQUEST

Ye little winds, I pray ye go
  And leave behind wild Banna's wave;
When dewy night comes dropping low
  Then keen around young Danny's grave.

'Tis he did love your salty breath,
  And when ye came with mist and rain;
But never with the scent of heath
  Ye'll meet him on the roads again.

No more his eye will seek the lark,
  Nor catch the primrose smiles in May;
No more he'll watch the white-sailed bark,
  Nor dream of countries far away.

The sweetest tune that ye might play
  Among the hedges that he knew
He'll never hear; for 'tis today
  The Heaven's choirs he's list'ning to.

JOHN P. BARTON.

GHOST ECHOES

Resonant oak, I will not wake
    One reed-thin echo of her name
Lest all your happy foliage break,
    Remembering, into flame.

The midnight oarsman in his skiff
    Surveys in fear the ominous sky,
And hastening past the haunted cliff
    Lets sleeping echoes lie.

HENRY MORTON ROBINSON.

FOR A DEAD POET

When some white soul, treading the quiet dew
That lies o'er your dead heart, shall come to you
And weep his great love out upon your breast,
I shall out-deluge him and love you best,
For mine shall follow you to where you are,
Through dew-starred grasses to the farthest star,
And evermore when I shall kneel to pray
Before the lowest step of God's white stairs,
My soul shall plead for yours, and all my prayers
Shall climb the dazzling height, and find their way
Through hosts of orisons to the King of kings,
Craving for you the joy your singing brings,—
All the calm joy and quiet, dreamful ease
Of your dusk-shrouded, peaceful, happy trees,
For that you kissed my cheek and called me friend.
Oh, that a kiss from man to Man betrayed
The Love of all the World, but yours has made
The world a greening place of song for me,
Eden with all its grace of life's Gethsemani
Its lark-song and its curlew-quiet end.

CATHAL O'BYRNE.

DEATH'S SONG

My bloodless hand today I laid
  Upon a fair-haired, winsome child.
She left her doll, sweet litle maid!
  And never after smiled.

Her eyes outrivaled April skies,
  Joy held her berry lips in thrall;
She looked at me in mild surprise,
  And followed at my call.

Tonight a yellow candle-gleam
  Showed me a miser, gray and old.
He wove him many a purple dream
  Out of his heaped-up gold.

He saw me in the doorway stand,
  He turned away when I drew near,
But he obeyed my swift command,
  White-faced from sickening fear.

I choose a beggar, now a king,
  A laughter-loving girl or boy;
And ever is their welcoming
  Devoid of mirth and joy.

Yet I am sent by Him who fled
  Away with me that saddest day;
To Him I kneel in trembling dread,
  He fills me with dismay.

One time I stood on Calvary—
  O blood-stained tree! A woful hour!
He fled His cross and walked with me,
  He reft me of my power.

WILLIAM V. DOYLE, S.J.

THE ABYSS

Even in prospect how the void of black,
　The depths of death appal.
The fingers clinging to the edge, bent back,
　Let go: and you must fall
Terrified at the darkness down, alone,
As hurtling down a well-shaft goes a stone.

Faint heart, consider!　Have you never smiled,
　Pitying the tiny fear
Of your adventurous yet timid child
　Who, though your hands were near,
Ready to catch him safely in mid-air,
Shrank back from leaping from the dizzy chair?

That little height to him a precipice
　Too dangerous and deep
For him to dare.　Yet much less lofty is
　The void you have to leap.
The abyss, you think?—no, but an inch of space
To your fond Father's sheltering embrace.

THEODORE MAYNARD.

THE OLD ROSARIAN

Fold her hands.　Ah me,
The wearied beads that she,
Though heedless, still would keep
Who prayed herself to sleep!

Simple be her bed
And symbol at its head;
And simple, too, the prayer
Both said and graven there.

Yea, let its letters plead
In words the young may read,
For such with her sufficed
To speak the Child in Christ.

Then be it softly breathed
As scriptures, ivy-wreathed,
Are spelled from off a stone
By wondering little one:

"The mother 'neath this sod
Played out her part with God
And so, in passing, smiled
When putting on the child."

Fold her hands. Ah me,
How cold her beads while she
Tells Mysteries, star by star,
Where Joy's and Glory's are!
FRANCIS CARLIN.

THE SHROUDED SLEEPER

Asleep, and dreaming God,
   He faced the Second Throne
   As one whose soul had flown
From body, bed and sod.

"Lord, while in the strife
   I own that I forsook
   The Tree, the Word, the Book,
And Crown and Bread of Life.

"The Crown of Life to be
   In this eternal Now;
   The Bread of Life which Thou
As Food didst offer me.

"The Tree of Life, the rood
   Above Thy altar-shelf;
   The Book of Life, Thyself
Besignatured with Blood."

Then he who dreamt him dead
　　Took on quick tears and, lo,
　　The Wounded Presence: "Go,
And sin no more!" It said.

Asleep, he dreamed till fears
　　Of Judgment wakened him
　　Who saw the morning's rim
A rainbow through his tears.

FRANCIS CARLIN.

SIXTEEN DEAD MEN

For the Irish Patriots of Easter Week
Hark! in the still night.　Who goes there?
　　"Fifteen dead men."　Why do they wait?
"Hasten, comrade, death is so fair."
　　Now comes their Captain through the dim gate.

Sixteen dead men!　What on their sword?
　　"A nation's honor proud do they bear."
What on their bent heads?　"God's holy word;
　　All of their nation's heart blended in prayer."

Sixteen dead men!　What makes their shroud?
　　"All of their nation's love wraps them around."
Where do their bodies lie, brave and so proud?
　　"Under the gallows-tree in prison ground."

Sixteen dead men!　Where do they go?
　　"To join their regiment, where Sarsfield leads;
Wolfe Tone and Emmet, too, well do they know,
　　There shall they bivouac, telling great deeds."

Sixteen dead men!　Shall they return?
　　"Yea, they shall come again, breath of our breath.
They on our nation's hearth made old fires burn.
　　Guard her unconquered soul, strong in their death."

DORA SIGERSON SHORTER.

"HOW SLEEP THE BRAVE"

Plain white crosses, row on row,
Across the silent hill they go;
Here lie the friends, and there the foe,
    Near to the gentle river;
Their graves are red when poppies grow
In summer, and white with winter's snow,
But they lie in close-ranked lines below,
    And they lie in peace forever.

With the dewy morn come the bugle-notes
Poured from a hundred golden throats,
And over their graves the reveille floats
    Of the larks, but 'tis thrilled in vain;
For sleep is sweet when a hero dies,
And sleep eternal has touched their eyes,
A dreamless sleep, they shall never rise
    To the bugle's call again.

When the sun sinks low in the ruddy west,
The farewell strains from the thrush's nest
Shall lull the sleeping heroes' rest
    In a hymn to the dying day;
There they lie, brave, dauntless, true,
Palled by the heavens' gold and blue,
And the rain shall beat a soft tattoo
    Where the warriors sleep in clay.

Plain white crosses, row on row,
Across the silent hill they go;
Here lie the friends, and there the foe,
    Near to the peaceful river;
Their graves are red when poppies grow
In summer, and white with winter's snow,
But they lie in close-ranked files below,
    And they lie at peace forever.

SIDNEY J. SMITH, S.J.

THE SOLDIER DEAD

There is a field where poppies blow,
And angels walking to and fro
Sing sweetly high and sweetly low
 For soldiers sleeping there.
They chant their orisons at eve;
At night when waking mothers grieve;
And in the morn when sad hearts weave
 New hopes to conquer care.

Within the poppies' crimson sweep,
Like weary sentinels at sleep,
The little crosses bend to keep
 Their tryst with those below.
Softly the angel-matins fall,
The far sky leans above them all.
God keep them till the last long call—
 At rest, where poppies blow.

HELEN MORIARTY.

TO HIS MOTHER

Nay, never weep,
For he hath won beyond all sad tomorrows.
His weary ashes sleep
Far in sweet France; his soul, assoiled of sorrows,
With unsuspected longings, leaps before
Unto his God. He lives, so weep no more!

I know.
A mother's heart
Is fertile still of tears.
Her griefs unbidden start
And she will not be tutored in her woe.
Her anxious love is very full of fears.
Ah, love must bleed and suffer all the years!
God made all mothers so.

But now,
Thy time of grief is over. He is gone
But is not lost. Nay, rather he has won
Abiding peace. Christ cherishes thy son.
There is a light of glory on his brow.
While all exultant ages carol on
He shall have naught but joy where God has put him now.

Ah, wouldst thou pray
To have him caught again in webs of care?
How serious and worthy was his way
Through a swift death to lasting glories there.
He won his goal with such a brief delay!

Wouldst thou, dear mother, have him once again
Take up the burden of uncertain years,
Give pledges unto weariness and pain
And be the toy of woe, the sport of fears?

Then leave
All bootless sorrow. Only pine and grieve
For those that knew no honor, faith and truth.
Thy dear one doth receive
For his brief dying an immortal youth.

Swift through the years to his dear arms thou'lt go,
For God hath planned it so.

Edward F. Garesché, S.J.

VESTIGES

TRIBUTE

What part has Caesar in that western flash
  Of gold along the sky's translucency?
In silver waters of the dawns that wash
  The coasts of day, what part has he?

If I am taxed by law because I bask
  In this pale beauty and in that strong splendor,
I stand upon the law, whose image ask,
  And tribute unto God I render.
                    CHARLES L. O'DONNELL, C.S.C.

GOD'S GARDEN

Very old is God's garden,
Very old is the earth,
Unvisioned its secret
Of death and birth.
Very old is God's garden,
We know not when
He began His sowing
Of the hearts of men:
To be ploughed and harrowed
By love, by hate,
For immortal gardens
Predestinate.

There shall come a spring,
When no man knows,
When shall wake the iris,
When shall wake the rose.
Each in his own appointed place,
For a day, for a year, for an eon's space.

Very old is God's garden,
And we know not when
He shall gather in harvest
The hearts of men.

SYLVIA V. ORME-BRIDGE.

HEAVEN AND EARTH

The trickle of the water in the pool;
  The light, reflected, flickering on the ferns;
The humming-bird's shrill cry; a beautiful
  New butterfly: these take my eyes and ears by turns.

These and a hundred other varying things
  A lazy man finds good to look upon.
I have no need to write a word, while sings
  A bird: my verse will do when butterflies are gone.

Some day, perhaps in heaven, when I am full
  Of wisdom, deep in God, when youth returns,
I may learn how to sing about the pool
  Whose light is now reflected quivering on the ferns.

THEODORE MAYNARD.

A PASTEL

Under swaying branches
  Clouded white with bloom,
Through a little garden,
  Splashed with sun and gloom . . .

Birds above the convent
  Singing heedlessly . . .
Apple-blossoms blowing,
  Drifting lazily . . .

Little crosses standing,
  Uniformly made,

Seemed to whisper to us
  "Years—like blossoms—fade . . ."

Then across the sunlight
  The Angelus bell—
Like a floating shadow
  Tinged with fire, fell . . .

Birds above the crosses,
  Singing merrily . . .
Apple-blossom petals
  Drifting, hazily . . .
                    MARY DIXON THAYER.

SUBSTITUTION

Now when the solid earth slips under your feet
        And all's undone,
Look up, take heart, the unchanging Heaven is won!

Here the rose fadeth, joy goes by so fleet,
        A bubble bright,
But to be blown on and to vanish quite.

Lay hold on things eternal for things brief!
        Nothing will stay;
Youth is a flower, withering, passing away.

Canker is in the rose, blight on the leaf,
        Rust on the gold:
The joy of earth a tale soon over and told.

Earth's for beginnings: there shall be no end:
        Time is not done
When love's drawn up to Love and both are one.

Here is your solid land; your lease is penned,
        Fairly 'tis writ:
Heaven's yours in perpetuity: seize on it.
                    KATHARINE TYNAN.

NATURE

"Our God is Nature, and Our Theology Evolution"
Helpless atoms—prithee, why now
   Should I "Lord and Master" you?
Bend a knee to gush and sigh now
   As your fond fanatics do?

Care if you evolve to measure?
   Fret if you should frown or rage?
Heed if you in some displeasure
   Quit your "work from age to age"?

Really, I don't care the slightest
   For your hate or constancy,
Be your fairest or your tritest—
   Both are quite alike to me.

Evolution, Devolution,
   Either way you're both the same,
And your might in my solution
   Precipitates to but a name.

All your moods are but reflections
   In the mirror of my soul,
All your graces and perfections,
   Garbs to fit your given role.

I esteem your stars and flowers
   In a decorative way,
And your superstitious powers
   Help give gusto to my play.

It's a pity you can't hear me—
   Constellations far on high,
I'll be talking when, I fear me,
   You'll have faded from the sky.

My poor heart too warm and small is,
  And my soul too palely spent,
Yet they're vaster than your all is,
  With its huge advertisement.

One swift thought can far surmount you,
  And a smile—but what's the use?
You're so vain I can't well count you
  Worth a thought's or smile's abuse.

There are wondrous Hands that bless you;
  You they laud, and Them forget. . .
But, your pardon, I distress you—
  So old-fashioned—my regret!

Nature, in our life your part is
  Of the smallest I'm afraid—
Go to chaos if your "heart" is
  Wroth at one poor verse I've made.

MYLES CONNOLLY.

I SHALL GO SOFTLY

I shall go softly, now, throughout my days—
Remembering fall of April rain, and June,
With scented lanes, beneath a crescent moon—
Emblems of youth in all its mystic ways.
I shall recall the tender wind that sways
Gray moss above a jasmine-sweet lagoon,
Where joyous morning climbs to golden noon
Filled with the birds' ecstatic roundelays.

Though softly through my days henceforth I go
Life's beauty still shall lasting solace be;
Each gleam of sunset gilding ancient hills
Shall leave within my heart a warming glow;
Each autumn-painted leaf shall gladden me,
And I shall joy at springtime daffodils.

LOUISE CRENSHAW RAY.

GREEN AND GOLD

Spring of the year, how soon shall you be gone!
  Flower of the field, how quickly, quickly fled!
Willow and elm, that now green raiment don,
  How soon your bourgeoned glories shall lie dead!

Youth of our life, how little while you stay!
  Youth of our life, with golden days agleam,
How soon your suns are set, how soon away,
  Vanished how soon the glamor and the dream!

Though green things die and time consumes the gold,
  Though through stark trees the wind of winter grieves,
Though life creep past ashiver in the cold,
  Yet had our youth its songs, the spring its leaves.

Blanche Mary Kelly.

SONG

For Harp and Horn

High traffics of the singing winds of morning,
  Great businesses of zephyr and of breeze—
The myriad cymbals of the wood give warning,
  Dawn strikes across the trees!

Hushed is the garden still; the daisied meadow
  Still dreams of cloud and star, nor hears nor sees
How swift, how bright, beyond its dewy shadow
  Dawn strikes across the trees.

Leap brook! Leap waterfall! The night is over!
  Begin again your song of distant seas. . . .
There is a sound of wings above the clover—
  Dawn strikes across the trees!

Charles Phillips.

CONSECRATION

I shall not ever love all things again,
Young saplings trembling in the wind's embrace,
Spring flowers, flushing with new beauty when
The kiss of morning lifts their dewy lace.
And never more shall I be wholly won
By the effulgence of a summer noon,
And elemental passion of the sun,
Or the white wizardry of midnight moon.

No more shall I be ever haunted by
The tonal mystery of high-flung seas,
Or lark songs quivering against the sky,
For I must now retrieve my love from these
To lift it chaliced, wholly pure, to You,
Since less than all would keep me still untrue.

CATHAL CANTY.

ON A SPRING MORNING

Nude trees against a rosy sky,
   Put on your lace of gold and green,
Till all the world shines like a glass
   With ecstasy from worlds unseen.
It is a blessed thing to rise
   In the quivering dawn of early spring,
And feel the laughter in the air,
   And hear the new bird sing.

Dear Lord, I want not anything,—
   Not wealth, not fame, not even friends;
Only the love that warms the world,
   The peace that comes when passion ends.
And what am I to share the sun
   And breathe the cool, life-giving air?
Lord, who am I to be alive
   And see Thee everywhere?

WILLIAM THOMAS WALSH.

LOVE'S GARDEN

I had a garden long ago,
  Cupped by the tender hills,
April-white with the cherry-blow,
  Blithe with the daffodils,
    Shadowed deep where the green leaves shook
    Cool and clear as a singing brook.

Scarlet of dawn and twilight blue,
  Night with her purple starred,
Dewy and fair His Feet came through,
  Sweet with the spikenard.
    Soft He came, and His robe as light,
    White as no fuller on earth makes white.

Lonely the garden, long ago,
  Pale are the daffodils,
White the bloom as the drifted snow
  Over a heart that stills.
    Hushed are the rills, unkempt the grass,
    There where no fragrant footsteps pass.

Lo, in another garden-place,
  (Deep where all depths are drowned)
Tears of blood on a haggard Face,
  Rose-red dew on the ground!
    Fall, O my petals, fall and fade:
    Here is the garden Love hath made.

                              ELEANOR DOWNING.

FIDELITY

I have lost love of many things
But not my love for singing springs,
For the cold beauty of the dawn,
The diamond dew on field and lawn,
The laughter of the sea and sky,—
Nor shall I lose it till I die.

I have lost love of many things
But not for yonder lark that sings
Above the swaying golden wheat,
Nor for the little furry feet
That slip past frightened in the dusk
Amid the scent of rose and musk.

I have lost love of many things
But not for all that twilight brings,
The tender silver of the moon,
The folded flowers asleep, aswoon,
The golden peace upon the sea,
The faithful stars that patiently
Keep watch above the slumbering earth
Nor vanish till the new day's birth.

I have lost love of many things
In my long lonely wanderings,
But not for those dear gifts that fall
Into the humblest lives of all,—
The rain, the sunshine, and the days
Filled full of work and prayer and praise,—
The pageant of the sea and sky,—
Nor shall I lose it till I die. . . .

ISABEL C. CLARKE.

JUNE

June! sweet month of hallow'd thought,
Binding our souls to Him whose Sacred Heart
Encompassed in wide love life's chiefest part;
Nor deemed the guerdon of our souls too dearly bought,
As with His Blood He sealed the Faith He taught:
Filling the garden of our lives with flowers so rare
That breathe the fragrance of His holy care,
With toil inwoven and with prayer enwrought.

Now in each garden bleeds the sweet-lipp'd rose,
Type of the mystery of that Heart Divine
Whose gift of love gave life to man,
And water changed at Cana's feast to wine.
Sweet miracle of grace when our new year began
That planted in life's garden a flower for all our woes.

THOMAS O'HAGAN.

A FLEDGLING ROBIN

Take us size for size and he
Is but a speck aside of me.
His gold-rimmed lip
Is but my finger tip;
His tiny throat—
A button on my coat!

Or take us age for age, and I
Am older immeasurably
By twenty years or so.
Three weeks ago
He was a wee, blue egg at rest
Under his mother's breast.

Or take us soul for soul; he knows
None of life's bitter, bitter woes,
No endless tears,
No agonizing fears,
No hopes of immortality
That ever try and trouble me.

Yet turn us both into a wood some May
Some fresh, fair morn and listen all the day
How very deftly he
Creates more poetry
With three soft-gurgled notes, than I attain
By a whole life of pain!

LEONARD FEENEY, S.J.

A SONG OF GRASS

To lowly grass kind nature gives
Most strangely sweet prerogatives:
Upon its cheek to feel caresses
Of all the south-wind's tendernesses;
To be the couch on which repose
The petals of a withered rose,
Or the loved object on which lingers
The tiny print of childish fingers:
To lowly grass kind nature gives
Most strangely sweet prerogatives

Nor fabled story can surpass
The simple chronicle of grass:
Grass carpeted the primal sod
Upon which Adam walked with God;
Its mouth drank deep the blood which ran
From the loyal veins of Jonathan;
And was it not Judean sward
That felt the treadings of the Lord?
No fabled story can surpass
The simple chronicle of grass.

WILLIAM F. MCDONALD.

A BALLAD OF HAPPY TREES

Many have sung of the Sorry Tree,
For sorrow's nearest to you and me,
(Though the Tree that was sad
Hath made men glad),
But none have sung of the Happy Tree
Save only me.

There was the Tree beneath whose shade
Mary the child of Anna played,
And the Tree that sheltered from summer's heat,
Good Joseph, resting his tired feet.

45

There was the Tree that made the beam
For the roof that lighted at Gabriel's gleam,
And covered from stormy element
Sweet Mary the chosen of God's intent.

There was the Tree to a manger hewed,
Cradling a God when men were rude,
And the Tree that grew in Galilee
Where He sat when the poor folk came lovingly.

But the Trees that joy did wholly fill
Were those He shaped by His Workman skill,
Hammer and adze and plane and saw,
Cut and chipped and hewn at His law,
Yea, to be wrought by the Master's Hand,
Happy beyond all Trees that stand.

CAROLINE ELIZABETH MacGILL.

THE TREE

Cypress tree, upstanding high,
Copper dark against the sky—
Tell me why you sigh and sigh
Always when I pass you by?
All the other trees are still,
E'en the poplar on the hill
Does not stir its silver leaves—
In your branches something grieves:
What have you to say to me
Murmuring, mysterious tree?

Long and dark upon the grass
Lies your shadow when I pass—
Unawares and suddenly,
Fearsome shudder chilleth me;
On my heart the weight of some
Unknown evil thing to come.

Leaves are singing in the sun
But your tawny fronds complain
Like a melancholy nun,
Or a wand'ring soul in pain.
What have you to say to me
Murmuring, mysterious tree?

"In a year and in a day
Will the Spoiler pass this way
Then my lofty trunk shall bleed—
And you cannot stay the deed.
They will slay me for your sake,
From my riven heart will take
Four new planks all straight and true,
For a narrow bed for you,
For a narrow bed and strong
Where you'll sleep both well and long.
This is why I sigh and sigh,
Always when you pass me by."

Sylvia V. Orme-Bridge.

ROSE IN THE RAIN

Fall, rose petal, fall;
  Your hour is done—
You have had your all
  Of dew and sun.

Now you must take the winds that burn
  And the buffeting rain,
Endure the storm, and learn
  What tears are, and pain.

Rose, rose in the rain, that drums
  Cold death on you, teach me
How to take death when it comes
  Bravely, unflinchingly—

Not grievingly, but strong and tall
  As you are, flinging off
Petal and leaf . . . how all
  The vanities you doff

Of color and pride, and face
  Held high, the flail
Of the whipping wind, the wild lace
  And lash of the gale!

Rose, rose in the rain,
  Teach me when I'm undone
To stand and to drink of the cup of tears and pain
  As I've quaffed the cup of the sun.

CHARLES PHILLIPS.

BLUE LARKSPUR

The white flame of a candle,
  The green flame of a star,
The yellow flame of a young moon
  Beauteous are.

But the blue flame of a larkspur
  Torchwise on its stem
Burning along the garden wall
  Surpasses them.

Who has not seen blue larkspur
  May look where stars abide,
At moon and candle flame
  Returning satisfied.

But who has seen will look at fire
  And in his heart will know
The pain of swift, unquenched desire
  For the flames blue larkspur grow.

SISTER MARIELLA, O.S.B.

PASSION FLOWER

They show the tenderest miracle of memory,
    These purple flowers that the breezes toss;
Year after year, each proud, unfolding blossom
    Reveals within its fragrant heart the Cross.

For even the flowers bear witness to His passion—
    The spear, the rod, the crown where cruel thorns met;
The crimson Blood, the purple of His anguish—
    Yes, even the flowers; only men forget!

MUNA LEE.

MUSIC

Wrapt in her own loveliness
    The young moon walks abroad—
Here, upon these trancéd faces
    Lies the light of God.

Yes, pure light of Him it is,
    This white reverence,
This white awe of ancient Beauty
    Wordlessly intense.

Music—Beauty's very breathing—
    Kindling cloud and air,
Bidding souls of all who hearken
    Mount and dream and dare.

Music—waning, falling, melting
    Faint and far-away,
Lost at last, and drifting blended
    With the moon-white spray.

Drifting past where mortal fancy
    Rears her last pale bars—
One forever with the rhythms
    Of the tides and stars.

ELEANOR ROGERS COX.

CANTANTE ARIOSE

Andante affettuoso

Milady Moon
 Has failed to keep her tryst.
I walk a lone, dark way
 While she rides with the mist.

Allegro gaio

One night ago, she walked with me
 Along the sand dunes where the play
Of waves made music for her feet
 And where she danced till dawn of day.

Ancor piu mosso

Grown merry mad, she scattered all
 Her diamonds upon the sands,
And laughingly recaptured them
 To span the sea with sparkling bands.

Adagio molto

Too soon, too soon,
 The dawn arose
"My love, don't go—"
 I tried to close
Her in my arms,
 But she had fled.
"Until tonight—"
 Was all she said.

Adagio patetico

The hedge looms black
 Where last night grew
Moon flowers brimmed
 With silver dew.
The trees that held
 Her spangled train
Like smitten ghouls
 Bewail their pain.

Andante affettuoso

Milady Moon
 Has failed to keep her tryst.
I walk a lone, dark way
 While she rides with the mist.

CATHAL CANTY.

MOONLIGHT

The moon reached in cold hands across the sill
  And touched me as I lay sleeping,
And in my sleep I thought of sorrowful things;
  I wakened, and I lay weeping.

I could hear on the beach below the small waves break
  And fall on the silver shingle,
And the sound of a footstep passing in the street
  Where lamplight and moonlight mingle.

And I said: "All day I can turn my face to the sun
  And lead my thoughts to laughter,
But I hope in my heart that I never shall sleep again
  Because of the pain thereafter."

The moon's pale fingers wandered across my face
  And the arm where my hot cheek rested,
And because of the tears in my eyes I could not see
  Where the black waves rocked, moon-crested.

ALINE KILMER.

SOLACE

No voice to comfort?   Is there not the sea's?
  That cadenced murmur of compassionate sound,
Most kind to ears grown old with clamoring,
  Or pinioned hearts in cords of silence bound.

No touch to solace?   Is there not the wind's?
  Healing with balm our fingers cannot know,
Brought from the scented, endless fields of Time,
  Tender with tears that trembled long ago.

No charm to liberate?   Oh, then, look up
  Beyond the ways of this infringing world,
To that exultant vision of release:
  The bannered sky with all her clouds unfurled!

MARIE BLAKE.

ENCHANTMENT

What loveliness a flowing river bears
  Upon its breast in quiet ecstasy:
The shining leisure of unhurried clouds,
  A peal of blossoms shaken from a tree;

Masts that have quivered to a thousand winds,
  Wavering rushes, and a sinking star,
The milky mists of morning, and unseen,
  The fall of children's laughter sweet and far;

Frail fleets of ice that never make a port,
  The breath of meadows drowsing in the sun,
A city's jewels spilled upon the dark,
  And swans that sail towards evening one by one;

And that dear treasure of men's fadeless dreams:
  Remembered bliss, old hopes that flamed and died,
The garnered longings of uncounted years:
  All borne in beauty to the ancient tide.

                           MARIE BLAKE.

YEARNING

As when a wave, most graceful at the prime
  Of its white splendor, when its lofty crest
Blossoms to foam, and breaks in fairy rime
  With mimic snow soft flowering on its breast,

Seems for an instant, in its slippery flow
  To pause, and yearn its florulous prime to keep,
Unwilling to rejoin the flood below
  And on that undistinguished level sleep;

So do the crested summits of our days,
  Some precious hours, so bright, so swift to die,
Linger, and with a wistful longing, gaze,—
  All beauty craveth immortality!

Yet be at peace! No yearning is in vain
   For Truth and Beauty! For one wave's distress
The sea shall bear innumerous flocks again,—
   And God hath infinite springs of loveliness!
Edward F. Garesché, S.J.

SEA MUSIC

The sun with its baton of gold leads the sea
And the winds in harmonious symphony.

There are light winds like silver-toned flutes that place
Aerial themes with delicate grace.
The deeper winds, breathing like throaty bassoons,
Answer their tremulous, querying tunes,
And wind violins, plaintive and sweet,
Catching the motives again repeat
In varying strains and harmonies
The exquisite cascade of melodies.

The waves are the basses, sonorous and deep,
Whose steady crescendos incessantly keep
Measured cadence until the volume of sounds
Bursts and like clang of cymbals astounds
The listening heavens and from their height draws
A ringing response of prolonged applause.
Catherine M. Bresnan.

RAIN

It rained today—
   And from their blossomy, scented hair
   The trees dropped perfume on the freshened air.

Blue shadows sleeping in broad market-places
Awoke, and crept away to narrower spaces.

A flush of scarlet from an oak-wood fire
Glowed through a doorway on the glistening mire,

53

And rings of amber sunshine circled o'er
A mound of dew-wet trefoil by a shadowy door.

The misty hills dreamed in blue ether, cool
As iris-shadows in a quiet pool.

Rood-screens of jade and pearl the thickets were,
Latticed with silver of Arachne's lair.

On a stray sunbeam a blue moth lingered
Above a bending foxglove, lily-fingered.

The common things, grass, mire, tree, quickening clod,
Were glad and glorified, and so, thank God—
It rained today.   CATHAL O'BYRNE.

STONES FOR HONOR

What kindlier fate has creature known
Than God assigned to simple stone?

To lie the daisy rows between
Cooled by the lichen's silver green;

To fence broad fields where sowers sing
Their harvest hopes in early spring;

Or, happier still, to shoulder well
A home where little children dwell.

Nay, some that solemn rite achieve
Which corner-stones of shrines receive—

But oh, the kindliest lot of all,
That may the meanest stone befall:

To feel Christ's Blood and Body rest
Serene against its altar breast.

If God loves stone so, what shall span
His prodigalities to man!
                    EDWARD S. POUTHIER, S.J.

ALWAYS A BELL

Always a bell to toll the hours!
    Into our hearts the wedge of time
Is hourly hammered deep, and life
    Is measured by its falling chime.

Always a bell to toll the hours
    In carillon or funeral knell;
The words of love, the dying breath
    Are shattered by a clanging bell.

Into the dreamery of joy
    Which almost seems, yet is not, real,
There falls a spectral echo of
    A brazen, desolating peal.

An hour is but a name we give
    To one of life's soon-wilted flowers,
And there will be, while mortals live,
    Always a bell to toll the hours!

HENRY MORTON ROBINSON.

AN OLD CATHEDRAL

I kneel but do not pray.   There is no need.
    My thoughts were graven in these Gothic walls
So long ago that speech would but impede
    A perfect prayer.   Cathedrals grow that way.
Each night I come to hear the phantom calls
    Of Saint to Saint go slipping through the gray,
And when they pause I watch the light and shade
    Entwining in the high-arched roof, or note
The gargoyles that forgotten hands have made.
    Again I am content to watch a mote
Of moonlight through the window's crimson glass
    Spill blood upon the altar's white expanse
To celebrate in silence Holy Mass.

C. T. LANHAM.

THE SPIRE

Thou art as lovely as the friendly mists that pause at dawn to drape
    thee in their veils,
And thou art strong as all the horsemen winds that gallop past thee
    on their neighing gales,
Mysterious as moonlight when it seems to mask yet show the beauty
    of thy face,
And fair as sunlight on the flashing frost that makes a silvern armor
    for thy grace,
Serene beyond the touch of time or tears, above the city's clamor
    and alarms,
And steadfast as the constant night that comes to hold thee in the
    silence of her arms.
        Oh exquisite and strong! Oh near and rare!
        My humble effort, and my soaring prayer!
                        MARIE BLAKE.

THE ANGELUS

The sun dragged slowly westward, and the day
Had cloaked the valley in his mystic spell,
As tender-throated on the air a bell
Chimed through the hush—a call on men to pray;
Soft in its pealing, like a robin's lay,
Chord overleaping chord in silver swell,
A cataract of cadence sweet that fell
To melt in muffled melody away.

So mute the breeze, it seemed a cherub's breath
In song celestial pulsed upon the air;
The blushing earth before her Maker's ken
Her veil of sable donned and wailed the death
Of day; then falling on her knees in prayer,
Adored the Word made Flesh for sinful men.
                        CLARE GERALD FENERTY.

A SONG OF ROADS

The world is full of roads that wind
  Over hill and hollow,
Roads that cast a glance behind
  And beckon one to follow;

Roads that loiter and roads that run
  Past the wild-rose hedges,
Roads that lure the wandering one
  Down among the sedges.

Now some roads take a brook along
  For the day's beguiling;
The brook is ever at its song,
  The road is always smiling.

Some roads go plodding through the heat,
  Dust-besprent and jaded,
Unswept by breath of meadow-sweet,
  By greening tree unshaded.

Some roads darkle and some roads shine,
  And some roads go a-Maying,
Some with the air of a martial line,
  And some like children straying.

And all roads lead away from home,
  Where the hearth-fire gloweth,
And every highway leads to Rome,
  And every lane—God knoweth!

But the fairest road 'twixt sea and sea
  That feet of men have trod
Is the bleak road of Calvary,
The rugged road of Calvary,
  That leads to the Heart of God.

BLANCHE MARY KELLY.

THE WALK

The little cares that fretted me,
  I lost them yesterday,
Among the fields above the sea,
  Among the winds at play;
Among the lowing herds,
  The rustling of the trees,
Among the singing birds,
  The humming of the bees.

The fears of what may come to pass
  I cast them all away,
Among the clover-scented grass,
  Among the new-mown hay;
Among the husking of the corn
  Where drowsy poppies nod
Where ill thoughts die and good are born,
  Out in the fields with God.

                    LOUISE IMOGEN GUINEY.

LITTLE WHITE ROADS

The little white roads that meander
  Under dales, over downs,
Loitering late by the hedgerows
  Hurrying on through the towns,

Leading to nowhere, and everywhere,
  Here, through a noisy mart,
There, where a thrush on an apple bough
  Tells all his secret heart.

Sharing the heedless babble
  Of a hoydenish, hill-fed rill
With a robin's quiet and vesperal
  Hymn on a window sill,

Resting by sunbright doorways,
    Scurrying past in the rain
Dark, cold houses, with finger on lip
    And blank, staring window-pane,

On through a blossomy meadow,
    Where a blithe freshet tumbles and whirls,
Weaving a web of diamonds
    O'er drooping fern-frond curls,

Oh little white roads! you ramble
    Through my heart, as you wind and wend,
And lead me, beyond life's mazes,
    To the country of God in the end.

                                    CATHAL O'BYRNE.

THE JEFFERSON HIGHWAY

By day
A ribbon of gray
From the arc at the east
To the arc at the west.

At night
Nothing at all.
Bubbles of light by two and two
Rise at the far horizon line,
Bubbles of light by two and two,
Always more and always more
Rise from nowhere out of the night.
They float along where garish day
Has marked the earth with a strip of gray,
Always more and always more,
Out of the dark from east and west,
Bubbles of light, their end, their quest
No man knows and no man cares,
Bubbles of light the blue night wears.

                                    SISTER MARIELLA, O.S.B.

IN GLENDALOUGH

I fancy now in Glendalough
  How soft the waters run,
While the singing thrush in the evening hush
  Looks out to the sinking sun,
And daylight high in the western sky
  Long after day is done.

If I were now in Glendalough
  I could be well content,
For what were the dearth of the barren earth—
  A heart with striving spent
Is a heavy load, and a fearsome goad
  Is a breast with longing rent.

No falling day there takes away
  The joy that morning gave,
While night unbars a flock of stars
  Above the dimpled wave,
And a spade would be a friendly thing
  Although it dug my grave.

CHARLES L. O'DONNELL, C.S.C.

INIS AINGHIN

I know an island in a lake
    Where blue bells blow;
Where quiet waters ebb and flow,
And on the cool, gray pebbles break.
In the wild ash the blackbird sings,
    The willow knows
A wayward wind that comes and goes,
Whispering of elusive things.
A place of peace, a place of prayer
    Is Inis Ainghin fair.

I love it for St. Ciaran's sake—
    Here, on this shore,
He dwelt a space, and evermore
Made of this island in the lake
    A shrine of silent, mystic peace.
Too exquisite its scenic joys—
He steered his bark to Clonmacnoise
And there he found his soul's release.
A place of peace, a place of prayer
    Is Inis Ainghin fair.

Its spacious solitude—so free,
    Calls me apart;
In noisy streets my hermit heart
Sighs for its green tranquility.
The world is fearsome. O I fain
Would be on Inis Ainghin fair—
There to lay down my care,
And to forget my pain—
Where quiet waters flow
    And blue bells blow.

SYLVIA V. ORME-BRIDGE.

IN GASCONY

In the hills of Gascony
The long, white roads,
The winding roads
Creep downward to the sea,
Through rose patches by crumbling walls,
And miles of military crowds,
Of poplars trim for the parade,
Up and down the waves of hills,
Through the great cathedral halls;
By the place where brave men lie
In quiet sleep,
In dreamless sleep,

While the stars and moon go by;
Where the day lives unafraid.

Along a road in Gascony
A gray old church,
Unsmiling church,
Towers in simplicity.
Stones that tired arms had raised;
Stones that ivy-fingers search
And wander over in parade.
Kneeling there, atop the hill,
Its bells of Angelus have praised
The Saviour through the centuries
Of fearful days,
And happy days;
Chanting the hymn of its memories
With gold-toned voice, and unafraid.

A Gascon village by the sea—
When day is done,
And work is done,
The sabots drop off heavily
From peasant feet, tired and slow.
Dim eyes watch the fading sun,
Unquestioning their life's parade.
Up the long road to the hill,
Where the top is white with snow;
Always in their simple faith—
They live in faith,
They love in faith,
They live, and love, and die in faith,
And watch the night come unafraid.

NORBERT ENGELS.

CALIFORNIA AQUARELLES

San Francisco Skyline

Dark domes against an orange west,
  A sharp moon swimming through the mists,
And down the northern shore a sky
  Clear blue, where still the wind persists.

Carmelo Sands

In one cool wave the golden green
  Transparencies that sunlight makes
    Under the locust's luminous shade:
In one cool wave a cloudy sheen
  Of veined dusk that floods and breaks
    To cataracts of carven jade:

In one cool wave dim lights asleep,
  Like violets under dewy leaves,
    Dreaming in opalescent gloom—
In one soft mellow cry the deep
  From flowery light and shadow heaves
    To curving crests of snowy bloom.

Point Lobos

Like the wide coolness of a pillared court
  The sea's smooth floorways run
Around the shadow of the darkening cape,
  Under the dusking sun:
Like a lost petal blown along the wind,
  Across the agate pave,
A rose-lit sail dips brightly in the breeze,
  High on a violet wave.

Presidio Moonrise

The sea-wind and the sea-fog build mountains in the west,
Wild peaks that range a barricade with banners on its crest:
The sea-fog and the sea-wind part, and with a silver sheen
The sea-wave and the sea-moon are shining in between.

Dawn and Dusk: San Diego

Quick as the waking laughter of a child,
  Sudden as windblown rain,
The sea-voice, murmuring in the gray of dawn,
  Begins its long refrain:
Soft as the gentle sleeping of a child,
  Light as a baby's rest,
The sea-voice hushes all its singing now
  Against the night's dark breast.

Mendocino Coast

Feeding the wintry hills with green,
  Veiling the sun's escape,
The white fog broods along the shore
  And hides the windy cape.
Against its bosom, soft as the breast
  Of a sea-dove in the sun,
The gulls skim down the darkening west
  And vanish one by one.

Santa Cruz

Bring me the silver of the moon, O Wave!
Come!—bring it up the sands you softly lave,
And dash it at my feet in melting light,
Flowing and vanishing along the night!

Noon at Monterey

A sail upon the blue, a little mist
  Upon the greening hill;
A bird voice on the wind that barely kissed
  The wave, and then was still;
A breath of heaven o'er the sea, a call
  Below—above—
And we possess the bright world, heaven and all
  My love!

CHARLES PHILLIPS.

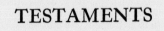

TESTAMENTS

MOTHER

I will arise
And go unto my mother,
Where as the ages pass
She waits to see
The loom of life its wondrous patterns weaving
And learn the secrets that it holds for me.
From her dear lips,
My name goes forth to Heaven,
From her dear lips so sweet,
So purely kind.
Her prayers have won for me my every honor,
And every laurel that my brows may bind.
I will arise
And in my gayest trappings
With every splendor
That my hand achieves,
I will go hence and by my mother's footstool
I will reveal the harvest of my sheaves.
If fates may curse,
I still can banish sorrow,
And rest again
Beside my mother's knee,
And with her arms about my weary shoulders
Await the worst the future holds for me.
I will arise
And go unto my mother,
And she will stroke my brow
With silken hand,
Yea, though the world should turn from me in horror
I go to her for she will understand.
The way is long,
The road is always weary,

And who knows
How much farther we must roam
Before we rest? But when my journey's over,
I pray my God will let me sleep at home.
I will arise
And go unto my mother,
She bought me life
In bitterness and pain,
And now, a man all sick with toil and sorrow,
I will go back and be her boy again.

R. R. MACGREGOR.

SERENADE

Sometimes you seem a star,
  Sometimes a wind-swayed flower,
Sometimes a lovely princess
  High in a lonely tower.

The phases of the moon
  In her white innocence
Give no such pure delight
  Or joy in difference.

Yet to me who love you
  No aspect strange you wear—
Familiar as my beating pulse,
  Vital as breathéd air!

Oh, once the starry sky,
  Oh, once the moon-bright sea,
Oh, once this blossomy earth
  Held bound my heart and me.

But now beneath your window
  Lost in dream I stand,
And I've forgot the singing stars
  And sky and sea and land.

JOHN BUNKER.

CANDLES

Dear, I have lit a candle for your birthday
Because a candle is so like to you.

What need is there of candles in the sunshine!
What need is there of love when life is gay!
But ah, a candle set within a window,
When twilight shadows come drearily gray,
Tells of a mother waiting with her dearness
To comfort hearts the day has touched with pain—
A little candle shining through the darkness,
How fearlessly it braves the wind and rain.

Dear, I have lit a candle for your birthday
Because in every grief I come to you.

SISTER M. ELEANORE, C.S.C.

COUNTENANCE

In those last days your face had grown so still
Against the rocker by the curtained pane,
Bright patchwork in your hands which strove in vain
To cease their fluttering and work your will.
And often in your eyes a listening came—
A small wind reverently stirred your hair,
As if a Hand Invisible rested there—
As if a Voice Inaudible called your name!

'Twas then I dreamed that you had gone away;
My heart was broken ere the dream came true.
Dearest, the sadness of remembering you
Through the slow watches of a year-long day—
That intent look of listening, poised prayer,
As if you heard His footsteps everywhere!

VERA MARIE TRACY.

69

THE IDEAL

I saw you on a stony pinnacle
With green and silver blossoms in your hair,
The chime of some far off ethereal bell
Was shattered on your cold white beauty there.
Your lilied body shone upon the air
With loveliness that sounded passion's knell,
And when you raised your eyes the proud stars fell
In adoration they could not forswear.

And as I saw you then I see you now:
A sweet cold ecstasy, immaculate flame,
Dispassionate, yet making passion tame.
And so I made this verse to sing thereof,
To tell all doubtful men and lovers how
You were love's discarnation, being love.

WILLIAM J. METER.

TO A LOST FRIEND

Although you do not seem to care
As deeply as you did for me,
And many friends now freely share
The love which once was mine alone;
I have a thing my very own
Left of our precious intimacy
Which neither time nor change can touch.
Put into words it seems not much,
Yet souls are born because of such
Glimpses of immortality!

I saw the look your young face wore
Upon an hour when deep speech lay
Between us two like sacrament.
I saw your face and nevermore
Can I forget! Peace! Go your way.
No newer friends can rob my heart

70

Of this. Youth has its own high day;
Nor lives there any human art
To lure it back or bid it stay.
In you mine is the richest part.
    I am content!

GRACE HAUSMANN SHERWOOD.

HALLOWED LOVE

Your love to me is like a secret shrine
Enclosed within a vast cathedral's walls,
Athwart whose floor the sifted sunlight falls
Through windows mellow with their prisoned wine.
Its Gothic pillars, in majestic line,
Enfold me with the strength of cloistered halls;
Across their peace your voice in music calls,
And yet, with head bent low, I make no sign.

Both celebrant and devotee, I yearn
To tell the flaming secret that I bear;
Long trails of incense, rising from an urn
Are spelling out your name in fragrant prayer;
Upon the altar lofty candles burn;
It is my love that I have offered there.

MABEL J. BOURQUIN.

TRANSMUTATION

Once loved is always loved,
   Fear not how far I go:
Night stars are implicit in the day sky,
   Violets in the snow.

And where you journey I shall be:
   Bread gives not back its grain;
The notes that have blended in strong chords
   Recur in the refrain.

Transmuted gold may not revert,
  Nor seed take back the tree;
The sun, moon, tides are not more steadfast
  Than your heart-beat in me.

POWER DALTON.

LOVE, THE MAGICIAN

Were every pool a wishing-well
  And every grove a haunted place
Where lovers, if they knew the spell,
  Might gaze upon their loved one's face;

Were every blade of grass a wand,
  And every elm a faery-tree,
And every hundredth grain of sand
  A charm to bear you straight to me;

I should not tarry in their debt,
  I could disdain all magic art,
Because I wear the amulet
  Of love's own magic in my heart.

HENRY MORTON ROBINSON.

TO THE COURTIER

I shall escape you though I tarry here,
You shall not know me howsoever near.

Your passing fancy was a pitiful art:
Who sees with fickle eyes keeps not a heart.

The tree that sang summer in leafy delight
Is yet that tree steadfast in winter's night.

You saw and praised me in an honored gown,
Yet beauty is truer in fortune's frown.

You prized the leafage while summer was near;
I shall escape you now the winter is here.

MICHAEL EARLS, S.J.

VICTORY

I sheathe my sword. In mercy go.
Turn back from me your hopeless eyes,
For in them all my anger dies:
I cannot face a beaten foe.

My cause was just, the fight was sweet.
Go from me, O mine enemy,
Before, in shame of victory,
You find me kneeling at your feet.

ALINE KILMER.

THE SHARPER PANG

What hurts my heart is not alone
　The thought that we never will meet,
Though I long to lay my love in your path
　To soften the stones for your feet;
But to know if I did that you would not care;
　That you'd wonder, in quiet disdain,
"Why should this stranger intrude on my grief?"
　It is that fills my heart with pain.

MARIE ANTOINETTE DE ROULET.

FICKLENESS

If spring winds were not blowing,
　Were nights not half so deep,
Perhaps, dear, I'd remember
　My tryst with you to keep.

But the white winds are blowing,
　I hear an elfin tune—
So I dance on, pretending
　I love the half-mad moon!

ELEANORE L. PERRY.

WHEN I AM DEAD

When I am dead, and through the final gloom
The tapers coldly light my silent face,
And men come to me from some brighter place,
Reverent on tiptoe through the darkened room
To take farewell, ere each his joys resume:
When such as these pay me the mocking grace
Of too-late lavish praise, that fills the space
Between the death watch and the close-barred tomb,

What will you say, uncomprehending friend?

Will you then know the meaning of the word
I spoke so often, and my little ways?
And will you give as guerdon at the end
The answer I so craved, yet never heard
In the long loneness of my living days?

SIDNEY J. SMITH, S.J.

DIVIDED

If I should come back to where you sit alone,
   Dreaming, it may be, of our better years,
O would I find again the look once known,
   The quickened step, the greeting surge of tears?
And would you be as eager to comfort still
   As when you petted me and ran to serve
Before misunderstandings came to kill
   Our peace of mind and all our days unnerve?

Is there late recompense for wasted life,
   For stubborn wills, and pride too quickly hurt?
Can healing surgery come with the knife
   Of old remorse?   O what can now divert
The mind from thoughts that pulse with stinging pain
   Of love too wilfully and early slain?

GEORGE LAWRENCE ANDREWS.

CHALLENGE

Your child mouth curves in a cynic smile,
    Your eyes are somber with fancied pain;
You're sheltered from every wind of life;
    Yet hold that life is vain.

Let the rough winds scatter your dismal dreams!
    Fix your dark, sweet eyes on the common way
Of toil and laughter. There you'll find
    Courage to be your stay.

MARIE ANTOINETTE DE ROULET.

UNHEEDED VOCATION

You should have walked those cooler garden ways
With others, whose low, sweet-toned voices drift
Across the silken stillness of the days,
And farther down, where twilight shadows shift.
You should have known the high, swift, rushing sweep
Of singing wings that pass by in the night,
And felt the palest amber call of deep
Far-gleaming prayers, from blue stars burning white. . .

You have not loved enough the garden ways,
And you have followed other voices now.
So, gaily, shall you dance on down the days
And never know the dear pain of their vow;
Your golden hair shall always glint the sun,
But lovelier far you would have been—a nun.

ELEANORE L. PERRY.

SIN?

Dim, twilight veils have shadowed your sad eyes,
And cast on them a somber, grayish light;
You cannot walk the days with easy grace
And carefree glance, though yesterday you might.
Now you must find a deathly, silent place
To breathe in, and your heart must wear disguise.

You were a happy child that happy day
I saw you first; your eyes were clear and bright
With the deep joy of living; and your hair
Was windblown carelessly. Your hands were white
And slender, and your voice silver with prayer.
You were an angel walking Heaven's way!

What have you done, my child?   Your hands are thin
And graceless in the cold.   Is there no gate
To answer things unspoken in your mouth?
What bitterness has cast you here; what fate
Has left you thus unloved, whose lovely youth
Was love itself?   What is it, child . . . a sin?

NORBERT ENGELS.

HIDDEN DREAMS

You will go to Astolat
    And I shall stay at home,
Watching the stars in compassed skies,
    While you the wide world roam.
You will see Sicilian dawns
    And I shall sleep till day,
Keeping tryst with weariness
    While you are free to play.
You will see old famous towns,
    And I shall only know
Radiant castles built by dreams
    Where you can never go.

HELEN H. SAYRE.

THE LOVE STORY

The invalid weaver of stories sits
    In her small white bed in her small dark room,
While across her enchanted vision flits
    Prince Charming of Nowhere, with sweeping plume.

76

But another Prince stands beside her bed,
   With magical mien and marvelous eyes;
She dreams Him into the story instead,
   And makes it a romance of Paradise.

With pen dipped in flame she writes of her love;
   Exquisitely beautiful runs the tale,
With tapestries borrowed from realms above,
   And His rose-red Heart in a diamond Grail!

VERA MARIE TRACY.

WHERE THE BROWN STREAMS RUN

Said I: "I'll go a-wandering, whatever people say."
Said I: "I'll go a-faring to a country far away,
For I'm tired of all the trouble and the things that must be done,
And I want some time for dreaming where the brown streams run."

Said I: "The city's noises I'll be leaving far behind;
I'll leave as well the worries that are moidering my mind.
Let the proud ones have the prizes that are all so dearly won,
And give me the quiet valleys where the brown streams run."

Said I: "My friends are many, and my foes, thank God, are few;
And I ought to be contented in this country strange and new;
But the dearest friends I ever had are buried many a one
In a little Irish valley where the brown streams run."

Said I: "Next year, the farthest, I'll be off as if on wings"—
But here's myself entangled in a thousand, thousand things!
And the years are slipping from me till their number's nearly done,
And I haven't yet gone back to where the brown streams run!

But there's another life to live when this one's over-past.
And maybe, by God's grace, I'll get a taste of heaven at last.
And perhaps amidst the splendor of that land beyond the sun
There will be a little valley where the brown streams run!

DENIS A. McCARTHY.

NORA O'CAHAN

(An Irish Street-Ballad)

Come all ye noble Muses nine that teach as many arts!
So ye may praise my own true love, who sailed to foreign parts
From sod the Saxon blasted with the blackness of his spleen
Till hungry hands of famine crowned the young British Queen.

In years agone my Nora lived beside the winding Strule
From which she walked, o'er Cappy Bridge, to Master Duffy's
   school;
With a turf beneath her oxter that was cut in Carrigeen
As a scholar's contribution to the young British Queen.

What little mountain land they had was kind enough for corn,
And on the skirts the cabin stood where she was bred and born;
But a patent Marquis neighbored them whose granted fields were
   green
With the grass their fathers sickled for no young British Queen.

And so this landed gentleman, who played the absentee,
Sent word unto his agent: "Sir, good Major Humpherey,
Take o'er O'Cahan's holding for his chimney-smoke is seen
As a cloud upon the country of the young British Queen."

"Come, Nora," said her father, "let ye pen what I indite:
'My Lord, it grieves me sore to learn the tidings that ye write,
Though what I have o' chimney-smoke be scant enough and lean
Since the praties failed to blossom neath the young British Queen.' "

O'Cahan, with a manly dash, he signed and sealed the note;
And when 'twas folded for the post his gallant daughter wrote:
"The Lord, Himself, of Abercorn, at Baronscourt, Demesne,
Adjacent to the barracks of the young British Queen."

But, sure, a fortnight hardly passed before the peelers came
With ram that battered rosy vines and horned the cabin's frame;
And while they quenched the fasting-fire, my love she cried her keen:
"Och, the chimney stones of Ireland on the young British Queen!"

"Now, Nora," said her father, "let ye hear what I've to say:
'Tis off we'll go, from Derry Town, to North Amerikay!"
And so they left what neighbors' hearths were still in Carrigeen,
To take their fated passage on the *Young British Queen*.

Good people, what is left to tell concerns my grief and shame
Who took a drop o'drink and woke with Private to my name;
For when herself was off from me, with bitter seas between,
I dreamt I took a shilling from the young British Queen.

Alas, the dream it proved me false as even it was true!
And Oh, my love, that I had left yon weary quay with you!
'Tis where I'd be but at your side beneath the billows green,
Had fortune let me perish on the *Young British Queen!*

FRANCIS CARLIN.

I LONG FOR SHIPS

The gray skies slant to the edge of the world;
   The gray winds groan in the lifeless trees;
The wan weeds wilt on the sullen earth:—
   I long for ships and the surging seas!

Whalers gliding out of Gloucester,
   Sailboats dancing in the bay,
Sampans past the Sacred Mountain,
   Proas paddled off Malay;
Ore-boats chugging from Messaba,
   Battleships no storm could tame,
Steamships rounding Madagascar,
   Chinese junks with sails aflame!

The gray mood creeps to the depths of my soul,
   The grim voice groans at my futile ease,
My sad heart sinks to the sodden earth:—
   I long for ships and the surging seas!

MARIE ANTOINETTE DE ROULET.

EMIGRANT

Take me where my treasure is,
    I'm sick of stranger lands,
The loneliness calls from my eyes,
    Yet no one understands,
The words I speak are wet with tears,
But ne'er a one gives heed,
Oh Erin, Erin, Erin, it is yourself I need!

The stilling, soothing hands of you,
    The voice that warms like flame,
The heart so quick to comprehend,
    The love so slow to blame,
Sure who that once has seen your eyes
Can e'er again find rest,
Oh Erin, Erin, Erin, till he's hushed upon
        your breast?

                                MARIE BLAKE.

FOR MY BROTHER WHO TOOK SHIP

You eat strange fruits and spices
    Brought far on wind-borne ships,
But still the Kentish cherries
    Are sweet upon my lips.
For you Algerian sunshine
    And desert-laden breeze;
Mine are the blowing branches
    Of rainy apple trees.

You ride upon a camel
    With steel against your thigh,
And thousand turbaned tribesmen
    Would keep your life,—or die.
But I, in misty mornings,
    Lug on my clay-caked boots,
And trudge through soaking grasses
    To hoe the field of roots.

I wouldn't change my place for yours,
　　But in the heat of day
I sometimes straighten up my back,
　　And brush the sweat away,
And rest a minute on my fork
　　Beside the mounting stack,—
I wonder how it feels to ride
　　Astride a camel's back . . .

MAIRE NIC PILIP.

THERE IS A DORSET ORCHARD

There is a Dorset orchard
　　With many a stooping tree,
And there in shadowed grasses
　　Once lay a lad like me.

And all that filled his fancy,
　　Or touched his heart-strings then
Were dreams of wave and anchor,
　　And ships and sailing-men.

And if the landward breezes
　　Rustled an apple tree,
He knew it for a signal
　　And summons of the sea. . . .

Now my wind-bitten fingers
　　Grow slack on rope and rail;
And sick I am of shifting decks
　　And mast and wheel and sail.

For in the long night watches
　　On winds that touch and pass,
I hear the Dorset apples
　　Fall heavy in the grass.

And through the blazing daytime,
　　When the waters pause for breath,
I'm thinking of the light rain
　　Across the Dorset heath.

MAIRE NIC PILIP.

COMPENSATION

A suppliant came to Heaven's portal,
  A stumbling wight in somber gown,
His was no haloed brow, poor mortal,
  He bore no palm, no laurel crown.

The gate, a single pearl, swung slowly;
  The stranger lifted frighted eyes,
How venture he among the holy,
  Rapt citizens of Paradise?

But who are these that throng for meeting,
  With songs, in dazzling vesture clad?
What deed of his has won such greeting?
  "We are the joys you never had.

"We are the love, the wealth, the pleasure,
  The honors missed, the hopes foregone;
Through us you mount unto your treasure,
  The Face of God, with veils withdrawn."
                    BLANCHE MARY KELLY.

CAP AND BELLS

I am a clown, a royal fool,
  A jester to the king,
I sit upon a lowly stool,
  And laugh and dance and sing.

Proud courtiers pass and look with scorn
  Upon my foolish ways;
I am a child of folly, born
  In sapiential days.

I flaunt my bauble in the air,
  And vent my clownish spells,
Before the face of them that stare
  Upon my cap and bells.

Forsooth, I should put laughter off,
  And don a sober guise,
The livery of a jester doff,
  To have them call me wise!

I am amused by their conceit,
  Pretense and pomp and show,
And day by day at the king's feet,
  A wiser fool I grow.

Some of them strut through his domain,
  As though it were their own;
Amazed, I note the frank disdain
  They wear before his throne.

No gold is mine, no purple ease,
  His smile is my reward.
I live my merry days to please
  His majesty, my Lord.

And He with favor looks on me,
  For He does not forget
The day beneath a bleeding tree,
  When He and folly met.

WILLIAM V. DOYLE, S.J.

THE SERVANT BOY

A servant lad am I
  Indentured by decree,
And 'prenticed to the trade of Him
  Who fashioned me.

From yielded echolings
   I brought my lilts about,
Who yet shall turn a marvel when
   My time runs out.

For though I've failed to word
   The wonder in my kit,
When I become the journey-man
   Who'll master it,

I'll make a rounded song
   Or spoil a crooked moon,
While cobbling at Sir Patrick Spens'
   Sea-weathered shoon.

Francis Carlin.

SONNET

I am a trafficker in smiles and tears.
   Those hard-won joys of which I am so fain,
   Men snatch from me and leave me only pain
For recompense, and bitter thoughts and fears.
No comradeship the day's horizon cheers;
   Joys are my merchandise and griefs my gain:
   My joys are fleet, but ah! the griefs remain
Through what brave singing of my lonely years.

Ay! this they cannot take, the gift of song;
   Shorn of all else, I bear the one great hope.
How cheerily then I trudge the ways along;
   With how light step and with what quickening breath
Shall I press on to climb life's ultimate slope
   And at its crest embrace the healing death!

Sidney J. Smith, S.J.

THE FOOLS OF GOD

We are a curious company, we fools of mother earth,
Partakers in the jest Divine that gave all being birth.
Who walk erect and unafraid our individual way,
Nor fret with what our neighbor thinks or what the world will say.
Our banner is a scarlet cloak; our sword a pilgrim staff;
Our trumpets are the pipes of Pan; our battle-cry a laugh;
Our captains, those fantastic ones that faced your mockings first,
The Master Fools ye put to shame and spat upon and cursed:
A king, despised of Michol, who capered in his joy;
A blind old man who begged his bread and mumbled tales of Troy;
A madman naked in the streets and shouting "I have found!"
And one who asked in vain for ships and said the world was round;
A shepherd maid who fed her flocks along a sunny slope,
And told a sneering, hopeless court of Voices and of hope;
A barefoot friar, robed in brown, who wandered to and fro
And taught his Sister Birds and tamed the wolf of Gubbio;
And at their head the King of fools, Who also knew your scorns,
Our King who bears a willow reed and wears a crown of thorns.

We are the fools! Because we sang when there was woe on earth
Ye struck our lips—our lips that drank the very fount of mirth.
Because we left the proven path from which ye feared to stray
Ye cursed us, knowing not our feet had found the chosen way.
Because our gaze was lifted up and bent on things afar
Ye called us mad, perceiving not our eyes had seen a star.

We are the fools, the madmen, subject to sneer and blow.
What do ye know of hidden heights, ye in the vales below?
Of dreams that wrap us in the night, and vast, untrammeled seas;
Of sudden beauty, strange and wild, and lonely ecstasies?
Our seat is with the Seraphim, the lightning is our rod,
Who hear the music of the spheres and see the face of God.
Tattered and scarred and mocked at, we hold a world in thrall,
And though ye scorn and hate us much, ye fear us most of all!

JOSEPH H. MEYERS.

RENUNCIATION

I am the runner that ran his race and lost.
   My brain sang and the air roared past my ear;
Through mist I saw the goal heave drunkenly
   All garlanded with victory—and so near!
When sudden, sharp with pleading and with dread,
   A voice rang at my feet, "O runner, spare!"
I swerved—and fell! My rival shot ahead—
   And I remember curses on the air.

I am the fighter who fought his fight and fell.
   The foe reeled and the fight was almost won.
I leaped to thrust when a keener point pierced home:
   The linnet of a woman's voice, "My son!"
I faltered, held my hand, and felt him grope
   His dim way past my guard, and in my ears
"Coward!" and "Weakling!" like a whelming tide
   Broke and shall break through the creeping years.

I am the lover who climbed to balconies
   More dazzling than beneath Verona's moon
Cast mellow madness on young Capulet
   Shrined in the arms of loveliness and June.
Sweet, ultimate surrender leaned to me
   Of all that lover ever hoped to win.
But a face thorn-crowned shone pale beneath the moon—
   I fled, and the waiting desert took me in.

God of the Course, Arena, and Delight!
   Behold him die, the outlaw thou hast made,
In exile—in defeat—and in the night,
   Alone—and *unrepentant—unafraid!*

                      Louis F. Doyle, S.J.

A HORSEMAN OF CHRIST

They ride with Christ their Captain,
  The cavaliers of God.
They ride in stainless armor,
  And high on silver rod
Each lifts his banner to the wind,
  And to the sun his sword.
They ride on glory's endless road,
  These horsemen of the Lord.

Now he is one among them,
  Who rode for Christ on earth;
Who quested with a knightly heart
  And with Franciscan mirth;
Who kept him to the saddle,
  Though ease-at-hearth enticed;
Who braved the highway's dangers,
  And rode for love of Christ.

Now he is one among them,
  A cavalier of God.
In mail like sun on drifted snow;
  On slender silver rod
He lifts his banner with the Name,
  And wears a virgin sword.
He rides with Christ his Captain,
  This Horseman of the Lord.

ALFRED P. SCHIMBERG.

CHATEAU-THIERRY

  O God, how vast
The distance seems to loom
'Twixt these heroic men and me,
High Priests of Liberty!
Unarmed, but unafraid,
Alas, I have no part,

But thrust aside
With lacerated heart
I watch the tide,
Undaunted, undismayed
Go rushing past
Amid volcanic gloom
Unto their crimson Calvary,
To set their brothers free.

THOMAS F. COAKLEY.

THE MONASTERY FOOL

Hey ho nonny, the wind and the rain,
Hey ho nonny, till the sun again!

So he carols, his heart that hungers,
So does he jest, his soul of thirst,
Hid in the exile with his Master,
Seems he last but is near the first.

Lowly the cowl and the faithful rule,
Laughter's sword has the cloister fool.

All the selfish sons and daughters
Goad the storms and sin's grim gain,
He has a song to turn the fury,
He has a King to be kept from pain.

Hey ho merry, with crust or crumb,
Let the wise fool beat his drum!

Midnight is the world that passes,
Fears he only the King's heart-ache,
Love he serves, and a sword of pity
Fights for the high noon to awake.

MICHAEL EARLS, S.J.

LIKE UNTO MERCHANTS

Like unto merchants vending vulgar wares
Are God's anointed poets, priests and seers
Constrained in faithless days to spend their years
A-hawking genius in the street. What cares
The mob for song or prayer or truth that bears
No tag of trade? And so the shame appears
Of talent pricing gifts and coining tears
To lay its table with unwholesome fares.

The pipes of Pan, the prophet and the priest
Are sealed by God in sacredness apart:
'Tis simony that they be set the feat
To barter brain for brawn. Men do not feast
On bread alone; they need both faith and art,
And owe a wage for truth no less than wheat.

M. J. RIORDAN.

THE PRIEST

There in the darkness, tense and low,
The whispering voices come and go,
And murmur tales of ruth and woe.

And he, no more himself, endowed
With God-like powers to heal, has bowed
To shrive them all, this shadowy crowd.

He knows not who hath knelt and cried
For sad transgressions, at his side,—
Some soul, for whom his God hath died!

He wields Christ's power to loose or stay;
Where red the guilt and horror lay,
He laves the clotted sins away!

EDWARD F. GARESCHÉ, S.J.

THE HARPERS

Beyond the wastes of misery
That haunt my dreams, O queen, of thee,
I hear the dithyrambic tread
Of harpers, young and nobly dead,
Chanting above the mourners' wail
A war cry sacred to the Gael;
Grief of my grief and blood of my blood
Harping the chord that rang from crag to flood
When death unclasped a steaming brand
  From Brian's unvanquished hand.

In Brian's dust and Owen Roe's,
The shamrock loved by Pearse still grows;
The tears of women Cromwell slew
Have drenched its roots with holy dew;
And when, like leaves in the morning gust,
Thy children scatter where they must,
Dark Rosaleen, their love for thee,
Arising chaste and terrible and free,
Shall burn on skies of blood and fire
  The face of thy desire.

WILLIAM THOMAS WALSH.

IRELAND

Beside your bitter waters rise
  The Mystic Rose, the Holy Tree,
Immortal courage in your eyes,
  And pain and liberty.

The stricken arms, the cloven shields,
  The trampled plumes, the shattered drum,
The swords of your lost battle-fields
  To hopeless battles come.

And though your shattered remnants know
  Their shameful rout, their fallen kings,

Yet shall the strong, victorious foe
  Not understand these things:

The broken ranks that never break,
  The merry road your rabble trod,
The awful laughter they shall take
  Before the throne of God.

THEODORE MAYNARD.

BANBA

A Gael am I—I soar above the star,
  Anon my wings with earthly mire are stained;
Alike I captain hosts of peace and war,
  I cast tomorrow what today I gained.

I am the ardent lover—and the cold,
  And none in all the world can hate as I;
And, like the brown hare, timid—yet o'er bold
  When high adventure sounds her thrilling cry.

I am the restlessness that never sleeps,
  And the dream-haunted sleeper of dead years,
I am the child's fresh joy that sudden leaps,
  Yet all of earth is bitter with my tears.

The world I ever wake to fresh amaze;
  My messages in sacrifice I trace;
Mine are the splendid, unexpected ways;
  I am the phantom of the God's lost race.

I am the patient builder—yet again
  For sake of one loose stone the whole I raze;
Truth-seeker, for perfection ever fain,
  I am the discord in earth's mundane ways.

The champion I of every broken cause;
  Not all earth's garnered fame my soul can sate,
And when the throng shouts loud in my applause
  I keep my tryst with dreams beside God's gate.

MAEVE CAVANAGH.

TO FRANCIS THOMPSON

The winds are all about me as I go,
Wild with the thunders of that nameless Name;
The blood-red moon grows pallid, cold as snow,
The stars, sere leaves across the heavens blow,
The sun dies out in glory, quenched in flame.

Ah, Christ! That feet must cling and cling to clay
While spirit, winged with vision, far outstrips
The thought-plumed seraph! Bitter is the day
And from the night is sweetness fled away: . . .
Sun-blind, I only know Apocalypse.

FRANCIS BEAUCHESNE THORNTON.

TO ALICE MEYNELL

Frost flower, frost flower,
    Snow-cold violet,
What did your Beloved
    When you two were met?

Ah! you need not answer,
    Through the dark I spy
A snowflake all on fire
    Hung in the western sky.

FRANCIS BEAUCHESNE THORNTON.

NEWMAN

Men found you subtle, master, blending skeins
Of taut silk thinking with the golden weave
Prayer finds in God. A stormy epoch's eve
Stirred your vast silence, till in flaming strains
You spoke glory. Yet deeper radiance gains
Who, listening close, can the still note perceive
That fires your music's heart—a note to grieve
And gladden, bred of the desert and swift rains.

Beacon of mystery! Soul's eagle, whose eye
Tirelessly saw through earth's hoar shadowings
The Undimmed Sun! With you these new years cry
For lighted ways and the dear morning's dew.
Hearing your voice, we feebly scan the wings
That made the peaks of sainthood plain to you.

GEORGE N. SHUSTER.

ON READING NEWMAN'S APOLOGIA

I saw the wonder of a living soul
Within this book. Its elements appear
As features of a face; high purpose here;
There faith as deep as death in rhythmic roll
Swells high in sequent waves, and shoal on shoal
The music of sweet words outpours; light-clear
Truth haloes every thought, and fear
No tittle swerves him from his purposed goal.

And then the anguish calling loud but brave
For balm of justice; guilelessly as child
Whom Christ set in their midst his worship lays
He at his Father's feet; his heart he gave
Entire and unrestrained and undefiled,
A glorious instrument of richest praise.

M. J. RIORDAN.

LOUISE IMOGEN GUINEY

A flower hidden deep where grasses high
Enshrined her loveliness in solitude,
That never might indifferent passer-by
Within the cloister of her heart intrude.

A harpist, playing half-forgotten themes,
Old songs that unremembered bards had sung,
Her touch caught harmonies from silent dreams
That long, long ages had not given tongue.

93

A lone lark rising high at early dawn
To shower song upon the earth until
In far celestial heights, on light wings borne,
The music sped and to the earth was still,
Its echoes now resounding in our ears
Like lingering melodies of other years.

CATHERINE M. BRESNAN.

MAURICE FRANCIS EGAN

He was a loyal champion of the Faith
Whose eager pen when malice sought to scathe
Or scar—alert in every sense—
Sprang swift, unfaltering, to her defense.
Who through the changing scenes of many ways,
The long and tortuous march of many days,
Tasted and savored life's true joyousness,
And dwelt not long on life's harsh bitterness.
Seeking the best of what in life he found,
His gentle chidings never left a wound.
Cheerful and hopeful, busy to the last,
Into the land immortal he has passed.

By Thine own paths from earliest youth he trod
To age—stretch wide Thine arms to him, O God!

MARY E. MANNIX.

AFTER READING IN THE SPANISH MYSTICS

There is a vision not my own, a splendor
That never flared across my darkened heart;
A sacred joy in which I have no part
Of passionate welcome nor of rapt surrender.
It is the vision, terrible and tender,
Whose images Teresa's songs impart;
The Spring from which Luis' raptures start;
The Radiance that Ramon's altars render.

94

Yet even I, the mute and cold, have been
Led by an echo toward the holy wood,
Where tranced and listening my spirit stood
Hearing deep praises thrill the fervent air;
And I for moments through the mist have seen
The star that glimmers on the lilies there.

MUNA LEE.

A THOUGHT ABOUT ST. FRANCIS

Sometimes when I am walking in a wood
   Where there are birds, I wish St. Francis, he
From his high station in the Place of Good
   Might suddenly appear and walk with me.
For then I know, in answer to his smile,
   The robin and the wren and every other
Would cease their merry singing for a while
   And come and listen to their Elder Brother.

I think it would be wonderful to see
   The lark drop down without the least alarm,
And the shy blue-bird leave the maple tree
   To perch upon the saint's outstretched arm;
To mark how even the sparrow for a space
   Would keep the pleasant woodland peace unbroken
To gaze upon the dear St. Francis' face
   And hear the words of heavenly kindness spoken.

To me the birds will never fly although
   I love them well and fain would have them come.
They seem to fear from my rude hand a blow
   Instead of what it holds for them, a crumb.
And so when I am walking in a wood
   Where there are birds, I wish St. Francis, he
Were at my side that, seeing him so good,
   They then might also venture close to me.

DENIS A. McCARTHY.

NOX IGNATIANA

His vigil was with stars; his eyes were bright
  With radiance of them.   Mystically slow
  Was their processional, while, far below,
Rome's quick and dead slept, fellows in the night.
These very stars had marched in cryptic rite
  For Virgil in clear evenings long ago,
  Gliding, like motes, athwart the overflow
Of splendor from immortal tides of light.

"What is this ant-life on a sphere of sand
    That it must drive, with ant-like cares, my soul
    Than all the stars together more sublime?"
So in the spacious nights Ignatius planned
  His spacious morrows—centuries his scroll—
  Upon a background of eternal time.

JAMES J. DALY, S.J.

VISIONS

QUO VADIS

Fare not abroad, O Soul, to win
　　Man's friendly smile or favoring nod;
Be still, be strong, and seek within
　　The comradeship of God.

Beyond is not the journey's end,
　　The fool goes wayfaring apart,
And even as he goes His Friend
　　Is knocking at his heart.

MYLES CONNOLLY.

THE TRAVELER

When my Love went from his house door
Where he shall enter in no more
Light and strange were the smile he wore.

My weary Love, lest he be spent,
Had wine and oil for nourishment,
Smiling he was and well content.

He had sweet oil laid to his feet
So they be strong, so they be fleet,
His heart and palms were sealed with it.

The saving waters on his head,
With words of life my Love was sped,
He lacked not wine nor very bread.

As in a vision he saw plain
The white table without a stain,
The spread supper for starving men.

The shoes of swiftness he put on,
My love he was so fain to be gone,
O, light and bright his face shone.

The night was cold and the way long,
With healing oils was he made strong,
And O, my Love, my Love is young.

And O, my weary Love goes light
Into lit chambers, all in white
My Love sits down this heavy night.

KATHARINE TYNAN.

DISTRACTION

When swarms of small distractions harry
  Devotion like the gnats that fly
Till prayers are cold and customary
  Not such as please Thee, Heaven-high:

When I forget for all my striving
  Thy presence holy and august,
Be Thou not angry, but forgiving
  To her Thou madest from the dust.

Say to Thyself: This mortal being,
  So deaf, so blind, so prone to sin,
Hath glimpses of Me without seeing
  The places where the nails went in.

Say: Through the crusts of earth, My creature
  Perceives Me, hails Me Lord above.
Rumors of the lost innocence reach her
  With full assurance of My love.

Say: Of all marvels I have fashioned
  Is none more wonderful and new

Than that this soul should go impassioned
  For heights beyond her mortal view.

What though her weary mind should ponder
  On small things meet for such as she,
O love! O loyalty! O wonder!
  That in the darkness gropes for Me.

KATHARINE TYNAN.

THE COMPANIONSHIP

God goes with me everywhere I go,
  So the joy of Him is never far;
Like the spring's breath to a waste of snow,
  Like in blackest night the clearest star.

O, the thought of Him's a water-spring
  In a parched land cracked with dusty heat;
Like green pastures where the dear birds sing;
  There my Shepherd guides my stumbling feet.

O, my God is dew in the starved day;
  Manna to the hungry soul and sick;
God goes with me on the difficult way
  And the thorn's a flower, the dead is quick.

Still His hand's reached out lest I should slip;
  Still His voice speaks comfort to my ear;
In our close, our dear companionship
  There's but room for love and none for fear.

O, my God forgets not: He is kind;
  He closer comes when the way is rough,
He shelters me from the bitter wind;
  O, my God is Love and Love's enough.

KATHARINE TYNAN.

SEEDS

I that am fashioned of the dust,
　That carry since my body's birth
Seeds of decay, wherefore I must
　Wither and fall and come to earth,
I carry also seeds of flame;
　Daily I feed them at God's pyre.
Spirit from dust when He shall claim
　We shall be mingled, fire with fire.
BLANCHE MARY KELLY.

CONQUEST

He said: "Come after Me."　But I: "Not yet;
My helm is broken and my banner torn.
My brow with blood, but not the foe's, is wet,
And all my stricken spirit is forlorn.

"I will go forth again unto the field
And do great deeds in sight of all the world,
I will make all to Thy dominion yield
And know Thy ensign by my hand unfurled."

So have I fought, but ever to defeat.
I am unhorsed, disarmed, spent utterly,
Yet hear, amid the trumpets of retreat,
"I have sought thee and not thy victory."
BLANCHE MARY KELLY.

GOD'S WAY

Dear Lord, You pleading asked a part
Of my already crowded heart:
And when with grudging, and with tears,
And thought of future lonely years,
I gave a part, ah, was it fair
To ask for a still larger share?

Ah, was it fair to ask a part,
And then with all a lover's art
To steal the whole? Ah, was it right
To use such sweet, tremendous might
Against a little, feeble soul
That feared the race, and feared the goal?

FLORENCE GILMORE.

REVELATION

There on a mountain top, I raised
My voice and asked one sight of Thee;
And my tongue tightened,
Full amazed
At my soul's crazed
Brazenness, and my speech, frightened,
Fled my throat, and my lips, dry
With fear, burned black, and I
Saw every neighboring tree
Crash—
But I saw thee in a lightning flash!

JAMES E. TOBIN.

IMMOLATION

We shall not barter souls for fleeting bliss,
And walk wide paths that lead to streets of gold;
We have not girded armor on for this,
Who take the bitter trails of pain and cold.

The shore-lights darken—seaward looms the storm—
The flowers we flung away were sinister-sweet;
But we have glimpsed a golden garden, warm
With wind and sun, that know no earthly feet.

For wisdom's eyes have beckoned; brushed by wings
That beat with mystic rapture 'round our ears,

103

The timeless tide of virtue, flowing, sings
The never-ending love-song of the years.

The buoys may sink, the channel-marks be lost—
Within our hearts the bells of victory chime;
For well we know, though sternly danger-tossed,
Our ship will make the port in God's due time.

We have not worn the sack-cloth, drained the gall
With joy, and kissed His feet upon the hill
For naught, and now we know that over all
There is a glory waiting for us still.

We have not quenched our souls in man-made bliss—
The greatest prize we won was in our loss;
We have but girded armor on for this:
That we might help Him bear His heavy cross.

J. CORSON MILLER.

DEEP WATERS

Should I launch out into the mighty deep
  Of Thy great love, and should I leave behind
  All else beloved, I fear that I would find
Myself adrift, and then, that Thou wouldst sweep
Me on and on, and round about me heap
  Such lofty waves that I could never mount the crest
  That towers above me. Foolish! fearing lest
He, the Author of those waves, should sleep.

Yet, I will bravely push my little barque
  Far out beyond the breakers and their roar,
Nor shall I heed the tempest, nor the dark
  Of sullen nights, for ever, more and more
My boat will bear me toward calm waters. Peace,
Then, and love, and of all fears surcease.

CAROL STONE.

THANKSGIVING

I cannot give
Aught to Thee save what is already Thine:
The breath and spirit's flame by which I live,
These, Father, are not mine—
Not even gratitude, till Thou dost bless
My heart and waken it to love and thankfulness.

And yet Thy heart,
That longs to hear me "Abba Father!" cry,
Contrives with infinitely generous art—
Such is Thy courtesy!—
To take with sweeter thanks than I can show,
As though it were a gift, the unmeasured debt I owe.

And when I bring,
Though grudgingly, some trifle of the whole,
'Tis not Thy treasury I enrich, my King,
But my impoverished soul,
Which, giving, takes again Thyself as dower,
And hides its gift where neither moth nor rust devour.

THEODORE MAYNARD.

IN HUMBLENESS

Lord Jesus, I have oftimes sued
To You, but now in gratitude
I thank You for my happy days
Of golden hours and pleasant ways.

I thank You for my life of ease
Under blue skies by tranquil seas,
For sun and stars that shine above
The common things of life and love.

I thank You that You gave to me
No fierce protracted agony

Wherein the body clouds the soul
In its long striving for the goal.

I thank You that when sorrow came
You taught me how to cry Your Name,
And in that moment You, my Guide,
Showed me Your Hands, Your Wounded Side.

I thank You that You bade me call
Your Mother mine, and knowing all
My need, You willed my prayer should be,
Mother of Jesus pray for me . . .

I thank You that You set me in
Ways so removed from lure of sin,
Not willed temptation should assail
One prone, alas, to faint and fail.

I thank You too that day by day
You drew me closer to You to pray,
Enfolded to Your Sacred Heart
In many a mystic hour apart.

You knew my little strength, and made
Life easy for me; grace and aid
Were never lacking . . Lord, I see
How tender You have been to me . . .

ISABEL C. CLARKE.

HOMO FACTUS EST

Love rose—for thus Love would atone,
And lift us up to Him—
Love rose out of the throne of God,
And down the starry spaces trod,
Between hushed choirs of seraphim
Alone Love came, alone!

Did not the stars grow faint, O Love,
As Thou didst pass them by?
Along the streaming Milky Way
Did not the worlds cry out, "O stay!"
And the great planets there above
Exclaim, "Lord, is it I?"

But, "Nay," Love said, "it is not thou—
Nor thou—I seek, fair star!
But to a little world I go—
A little world thou dost not know—
The way to it is very far,
And I am weary now . . ."

Did not the flaming suns turn white
With sudden jealousy?
Did not the proud fixed stars display
Reflected glory, ray on ray,
Each crying, "Rest, O rest on me!
Behold how soft my light!"

Yet in the corridors of space
Love did not hesitate—
On starry breasts He did not rest,
But hastened on upon Love's quest,
And comets—meeting Him—were late
At their appointed place.

Then Love unto our earth drew near—
Our little earth that lies
So tangled in the thread of years,
So stained with human blood and tears—
And to the wonder of the skies
Love said, "I shall pause here."

MARY DIXON THAYER.

THE LITTLE GIFT

O! With a gesture light and free,
Lord, I would give my life to Thee—
Not solemnly,
Not grudgingly.

No! I would take my life and fling
It at Thy feet, and sing, and sing,
So I might bring
Thee this small thing!

MARY DIXON THAYER.

PETITION

My little lamp is almost empty, Lord;
    The light is dim.
Fill it with sacrificial oil of pain,
    Up to the brim.
Wash it with tears 'til crystal clear it shines;
    Trim the wick right:
Then touch it with Thy love and it will give
    Beautiful light.

RUTH MARY FOX.

CONFESSION

I've bowed my head at last,
    And I had held it high;
For pride, so great in past
    Was very loath to die.

And now my will be Thine.
    I've learned through bitter loss,
That prouder heads than mine
    Have bent to kiss the Cross.

HELEN R. KAHN.

A PRAYER

Not to be loved—nay, but to love,
I ask, O Lord!
Pierce Thou my heart with love as with
A shining sword
Plunged deep into this heart—plunged to
The jewelled hilt,
Nor do Thou draw it forth until
My life is spilt!

Not that I may feel Thy love,
O Lord, for me,
But that I may prove unto death
My love for Thee.
Not that I may Thy sweetness know,
And Thy caress—
Nay, but to give, O Lord, I ask—
Not to possess!

MARY DIXON THAYER.

THANKS GIVEN

There is so much to thank Thee for,
  Thy favors are so great,
My heart seems breaking, dear my Lord,
  Beneath their precious weight.

I thank Thee then for these my eyes,
  My happy eyes that see
The beauty in the silver rain,
  The May mist on the sea.

I thank Thee, Lord, that I can hear,
  With breathless joy, a song,
And draw it to my very heart
  And hold it all day long.

I thank Thee, too, that I can walk
  Beneath the skies at night,
Through scented streets where spring has passed
  With robes of starlit white.

I thank Thee, O Thou Crucified,
  That I have known the pain
Of giving what I longed to keep,
  That theirs might be the gain.

I thank Thee, Lord, that I have loved,
  With all my poor heart's best,
And never once the trust betrayed
  Each dear love strangely blest.

I thank Thee, Lord, Oh most of all,
  For this sweet sense of Thee,
This blessed sense that fills me through,
  With singing ecstasy.

ELEANOR M. LEARY.

PRAYER FOR COMPLINE

Wayward, at evening I turn me home.
  The wraiths have vanished, withered are the flowers
  That led me straying through the truant hours;
Wearied and hungry to Thy side I come.
And when upon Thy knees I tender all
  My hard-won gains for favor in Thy sight,
  Their value measured in Thy clearer light,
The day's dead treasures from my fingers fall.

With what high hopes, what noble longings fired,
  The morning sped me forth upon my quest!
    My child heart hath betrayed me. Far at noon
    My faltering footsteps led, and all too soon
Night brings me to Thee, penitent and tired.
  Father, forgive, receive me. I would rest.

SIDNEY J. SMITH, S. J.

TEMPTATION

Like a strident music
    Struck from a passionate hand,
Like to a storm in its fury,
    Lashing the lonely strand.

Like to a surging ocean
    Thundering anthems deep,
Like to a shuddering forest
    Startling the night from its sleep.

Only God in Heaven,
    Meeting this wild unrest,
Can still the ache, the tumult,
    The torture of my breast.

CAROLYN RUTH DORAN.

SILENT GRIEF

I have buried my heart so deep in earth
That none can find it for sorrow or mirth,
And none can claim it for hers or his—
Only the Crucified knows where it is.

Only His infinite gaze can sweep
The hidden graveyards where souls lie deep—
Only His heart can catch the sound
Of sobs where tears run underground.

CAROLYN RUTH DORAN.

"LORD, IT IS GOOD FOR US TO BE HERE"

Thou art alone on Thy Cross, my Lord,
    And I am alone at Thy feet.
Yet it is good it should be so,
    And oh, it is bitter sweet!

My arms are bruised from pressing close,
    The wood of Thy cross is hard,

111

And Thou wouldst bend down to comfort me
    But they nailed Thee fast, my God!

And yet it is good it should be so
    And oh, it is bitter sweet,
To give my hurt for Thy dear love
    And kiss the wounds of Thy feet.

                        ELEANOR M. LEARY.

ATTAINMENT

Let me go back again. There is the road,
O memory! the humble garden lane
So young with me. Let me rebuild again
The start of faith and hope by that abode:
Amend with morning freshness all the code
Of youth's desire; remap the chartered main
With tuneful joy, and plan a far campaign
For prouder marches in ambition's mode.

Ah, no, my heart! more certain now the skies
    With joy abide. The cage of tree and sod,
        Horizons firm that faith and hope attain,
Far realms of innocence in children's eyes,
    And hearts harmonious with the will of God,—
        These might I miss if I were back again.

                        MICHAEL EARLS, S. J.

THE DARK'S MUSIC

Thy sorrows can find laughter; dreary places
    Know it. On blackest marsh the lilies fling
    A radiant smile, like starlight burgeoning
Brightest where deeper seem the midnight spaces.
What silvern sound anon! To voiceful graces
    The rainy roofs are tuned, and chimneys bring
    Flutes of the wind, like memories that sing—
Oh, the far youth!—sweet words no length effaces.

Look deeper still, strike flinty gloom amain.
  The desert rock obeyed the rod of Moses
  In cooling streams: and thou shalt wear as roses
The bruising thorns—thy bleeding hope's refrain;
  From music, more than marshy night discloses,
Rise the brave words across thy lips of pain.

MICHAEL EARLS, S. J.

REQUIEM

Out of the silence, the wind,
Out of the darkness, the stars,
Into the cold earth the corpse, the corpse—
    Ah, never mind!

Out of my labor, my mirth,
Out of anxiety, peace;
Out of the cold grave my soul, my soul,
    Shedding his earth.

Out of my sinning, despairs,
Out of my penance, my hope,
And my new soul weaving, weaving
    A robe from your prayers.

WILLIAM THOMAS WALSH.

PRAYER

(To be said when putting on one's coat)

Keep Thou, O Lord, my going out,
  And keep Thou, too, my coming in;
With Thy love compass me about
  To keep me safe and free from sin.

Bless Thou my going out, and bless
  All those whom I may chance to meet;
Wherever I go, let men confess
  That Thou art good, and virtue sweet.

Bless Thou my coming in; and when
    I come, come Thou, dear Lord, with me
That men may feel Thee near—and then
    Bless all the gathered company.

Bless me and this garment which I wear
    When I go out, when I come in;
Forth then into the world I'll fare
    And come back safe and free from sin.

RUTH MARY FOX.

WAY OF ALL SHIPS

Short as a shower are the lyric days
    Of primal promise and heroic mood,
When life is yet a ship upon the ways
    And love is making music in the blood.
Ah, what a sodden compromise we make!
    How shamefully we acquiesce, enthralled
By dingy cargoes—we who meant to take
    Nothing but freights of gold and emerald.

To no star true, we are by self betrayed;
    We give a kingdom and receive a crust;
The salt of life, the wine of song we trade
    For bilge and seaweed, barnacles and rust.
Until above the keel our first strength laid
    The tattered canvas moulders into dust.

HENRY MORTON ROBINSON.

THE TWO MIRACLES

A flame caught in a flame, a flame white-burning
    Beneath the outer flame's enveloping,
Is the irradiate soul, for ever yearning
    Out the half-glooms of vision's prisoning,
To look into life's spacious heart at will
And scan more deeply beauty's miracle.

A flame caught in a flame, and calmly burning
  Beneath the vesture of the outer wraith:
So lives the soul of beauty, ever turning
  Unto the eye that gazes with love's faith.
And secret kinship draws impalpable
The miracle a-near the miracle.

But though a gleam, perpetually shining,
  Sweep lambent through the heavens' mysteries;
Haunt the intricacies of earth's designing;
  Flicker athwart the tissue of the seas;
Drift through life's flame,—yet veiled, intangible
As truth, is the full-radiant Miracle.

P. J. O'CONNOR DUFFY.

LOST DREAMS

I miss the happy, wistful dreams
  I loved to dream long, long ago;
Since they are lost the charm is fled
From silent stars, and whispering streams,
  And half the lovely things that grow.
I cannot weave my dreams anew,
Because, alack! they've all come true.

FLORENCE GILMORE.

NEED

Why should one crave a blossoming tree,
  What is it to such as I
If peach boughs burn incredibly
  And flaming petals fly?

Petals might spread a fragrant bed
  Sweeter than any down.
Weave a fillet for the head,
  Or a lovely gown,

115

But what of the loaf for winter,
And coverlet, the same?
What is peach-blossom hunger,
That need one cannot name?

POWER DALTON.

FAILURE

A candle burning in ghoul-haunted halls,
Trembling afraid before the monstrous forms
Itself begets upon the cobwebbed walls,
Half-smothered by the ghosts of long-spent storms
That held their orgies, danced their bacchanals
Within these moss-grown ruins of the past;
A candle burning, that flickers, flames, and falls,
That fails and flares, and gutters out at last.

Such was my poor ambition, a pale, wan light
That feared the shadow doubts itself begot,
That knew myself too weak, too puny, frail. . . .
That fought awhile for what it knew was right,
That dreamed great dreams . . . but cowardly forgot
The Power above myself that cannot fail.

RICHARD F. GRADY, S.J.

REMNANTS

I have made a little world
From things such as I,
Cast aside as broken
And destined to die.

I have built a little house,
Carefully and long,
With ugliness outside
And inside . . . . song.

I have made a Joseph's Coat,
 Colorful and thin,
With patches of beauty
 Sewed wrong-side in.

And when I walk at high noon
 Through the market place,
I thank the God that gave me
 A long, straight face.

C. T. LANHAM.

RECIPROCITY

At last life comes to fit me
 Like a well-worn shoe
With the outer heel run over
 And the sole half through.

It was difficult in breaking.
 It pinched. It cracked. It squeaked.
And there never was a shower
 But the poor thing leaked.

I wore it . . . well, I had to . . .
 There was no exchange you see.
But at last I shape into it
 And it shapes over me.

C. T. LANHAM.

CHINESE LANTERNS

My loves are chinese lanterns strung across
 The gradual garden of my years. Now night
Is come, how gallantly they twirl and toss
 With every tremor of the wind, each light
Contriving arabesques across the dark
 Unruffled pool of dead desire! How brave
Are these small lamps to strive against the stark
 Reality of time, the bridal grave,

117

And even Him to whom I pledged my fast
  Allegiance.   There is little left to do
But watch my chinese lanterns in their last
  Fantastic dance drive colored daggers through
The nerveless night, and when the dance is done
To wait their quiet quenching, one by one.
C. T. LANHAM.

SEAWARD

Let me go seaward . . . softly . . . alone . . . and die.
  Let my soul sweep up like a swift-winged swallow and pass.
Let my soul swerve up like a blue smoke in a windy sky,
  And where I have walked . . . let the rain ruffle the grass.

Let me go seaward, God, . . . broken and blind . . .
  Ancient of grief and of gray and scarlet song.
Let me go seaward as the sandaled wind
  And the red and yellow leaves, feeling no bitter thong

Of beauty cutting through my weary throat,
  Let me go seaward, God, deaf to the old, old
Trumpetings of life . . . hearing only one high note
  Of Yours piercing the silence like a lance of gold.
C. T. LANHAM.

LET MY SOUL BE A TRUMPET

Let my soul be a trumpet sounding
  The radiant love of the Lord;
Forever at locked gates pounding
  With the force of the living word.

Let my soul be a slim flute, singing
  Bright airs in the dark of the sod,
Recalling the White Dove winging
  From the wonderful Mind of God.

118

Let my soul be a green tree blowing
   In the cold, gray paths of the rain,
So that men may be gladdened for knowing
   The beauty that springs from pain.

Let my soul be a lily of whiteness,
   Spread peerlessly pure in the morn,
To dazzle the world growing sightless
   To things that are spirit-born.

And then at the last let my soul—
   Intangible spark of desire—
Be blown to its ultimate goal:
   God's bosom of fire.

J. CORSON MILLER.

QUEST

I go to seek
   What none may find
Beyond the reaches
   Of the wind,—
A breath of song,
   The sunset's gold,
The secret word
   The winds have told.

I go to seek
   What none may know
Who walks the ways
   Of life and woe,—
The raptured singing
   Of a bird,
That never ear
   Of man has heard.

I go to seek
    What none may see,—
The hidden heart
    Of mystery;
Though I shall not
    Attain my goal,
My questing feeds
    My seeking soul.

                    EDGAR DANIEL KRAMER.

RECOMPENSE

Out of this clamor of the slakeless rain
Shall come white splendor in a sodden field;
The wind shall shout no longer, and shall yield
To night-soft singing in the trees again.
Out of this rending of the sky in twain
By lurid lightnings shall the sun shine through,
And lure the lark to carolings anew,
And urge the thrush to tempt its latent strain.

Out of this tumult of my soul shall come
A sudden peace I had not dared to know;
A joy shall rise when my vexed lips are dumb
And I shall laugh that I had grieved me so
O'er pain that is not pain since I have learned
That beauty lurks within the things I spurned!

                    EMILE KESSLER.

LIKE GROPING CHILDREN

Like the wee child that, toddling at my side,
    Unconscious of the dangers of the way,
Disdains all help and laughs with baby pride
    At his achievement, then, in great dismay,
Views the great breach or stumbling-block before;
    His hand is raised in trusting search for mine,
And, finding it, he is afraid no more,
    Nor wanders aimless; so, without design,

120

In vague unrest, by every beck and nod
　　Of fame and pleasure lured, forgetful quite
Of His great nearness,—so I walked with God,
　　Until, in dire distress and groping fright,
I sought His hand.　Content, no more alone,
All times I feel its pressure in my own.

VERA V. HOENE.

NEW LITANY

If we were faithless
We'd walk as fools walk,
Swaying, witless,
Through life's brief day;

Lifting pallid voices
In feeble small talk,
Being inarticulate
Holily to pray;

Having for soul
Whatever a beast has,
Nothing to dream of,
Nothing to mourn;

Visioning shrouded
In stark existence,
Vagrant wayfarers,
Purposeless, forlorn.

Lord God, deliver us
From hapless byway,
Creeds indeterminate,
Babylon, rue.

Lord, have mercy!
Keep us in Thy way,
High hearts singing
Faith that is true!

CAROLYN RUTH DORAN.

YOUR SELVES

You stand in a great room
  Where a pier-glass
Towers on either side of you;
  Where there rippling pass
Like a silver river
  Dim in tree-shade,
All the days, all the years
  That were ever made.

Far down that distance
  You can see go
As many selves of you
  As your heart may know,
As many dim decisions
  As your years have held,
From memory receding
  Into times of eld.

Between dim mirrors
  Of the years you stand,
Your many selves reflected
  On your right and left hand.

ISABEL FISKE CONANT.

IN HOSPITAL

Here through long days their broken forms have lain.
  To whose weak, fearful lips is lifted up
  The Grail of Suffering, the brimming cup
Of gall and myrrh, their sacrament of pain.
Surcease from agony they have not known;
  With pangs they tell the long slow hours of light
  And stars more slowly wheeling through the night,
Yet dawn still finds them suffering alone.

From His high wall to whence low moanings start,
  The white-swathed Calvary where each one lies
    Bearing His Stigmata on limbs and heart,
The Crucified turns His great sad pitying eyes;
  Whom at the last He dowers with sweet release,
    Upborne on healing wings of pain and peace.

SIDNEY J. SMITH, S.J.

A SMITTEN LEVITE'S CHALLENGE

O Death and did you think to frighten me
When hungrily you hung about my bed?
Ah! knew you not I have a destiny?
See! there it is upon the altar-stone,
That flashing Cup that waits my anxious touch,
That Vintage calling my poor lips
To drink its honeyed depths!
Now leave me, Death, take off your fevered breath.
I must, oh yes, I must go on.
I have a destiny.
But years from now when I have run my course,
Fulfilled the task God put into my hands,
Then come, I'll greet you graciously.
Unmurmuring I'll clasp your hand and go.

HARRY P. WALSH.

DOUBT

Across the levels of a desert waste,
  Beneath the arrows of the zenith light,
    My soul, like panting eaglet, wheels its flight
Alone and desolate.   No course is traced
For me; no guiding buoys I spy emplaced
  Upon the heaveless waves of sand.   I sight
    No luscious isles to rest among, no white
Cool surf to which my weary wings may haste.

Had I but faith how swift amid the gloom
  Of blazing sun and dunes of blistering sand,
    Might I find flashing pools of waters sweet,
And gardens fainting with the glorious bloom
  Or rose and asphodel in Eden-land
    That now hath only flint for naked feet.

M. J. RIORDAN.

BEAR YE ONE ANOTHER'S BURDEN

I wonder if no friends were left to me
  How I should fare;
How brave the world and all its misery
  With none to care.

The doom is not that friendless and alone
  We earn our bread;
For that were but to turn our hearts to stone,
  Our feet to lead.

It was but meant that friend with friend we go
  Adown the road;
That humbly hand to hand we work, and so
  To share the load.

Then let me not, dear Lord, forget the plea
  Each dawning day,
That altogether lone I may not be
  To face the fray.

M. J. RIORDAN.

COURAGE

A porcelain tall thing of melting lines,
  She held it tightly all a summer's day,
And thrilled to see its changing shadows flow
  As lithe as twining tiger-cubs at play.
A satyr screamed—a cry—in silly shards
  About her startled feet the fair vase lay.

124

The satyr laughed and fled. Too deep in pain
   To care, she garnered all the bits of blue,
Her fair hair in the dust. She sought no aid
   But labored weary days and wan nights through
Until with tears and blood 'twas whole again
   And from its heart tall, queenly lilies grew.

Louis F. Doyle, S.J.

DEPARTURE

The last goodbye was said, the last friend gone:
   Then, as the shimmering mist of sunset fell
Over the city, I went out alone
   To say farewell to London, and farewell
To her dear river. To a million homes
   Surged by the happy crowds, nor marked me there
Weeping while gazing on the towers and domes
   Wren poised so proudly in that tender air.

To these farewell! Farewell to Edward's shrine
   And Bentley's campanile! My adieu,
My holy city!—yet no longer mine,
   Since now my exile must begin anew.
Parting, I print your features on my brain,
Mother, whose face I may not see again.

Theodore Maynard.

I WAS IN PRISON AND YOU VISITED ME NOT

You pass Me by, you do not glance
   To see if I be there or no,
The world of pomp and circumstance
   Calls eagerly, and on you go.

You quest the ages near and far
   To find the gifts I offer you.

125

Of hopeless days, and griefs that mar
　　You weave a crown of bitter rue.

You bear within you cankers deep,
　　Oh weary hearts, masked by a smile,
I, watching, slumber not nor sleep,
　　Oh come and rest in Me awhile.

Oh look, you heedless, if there be
　　Sorrow like to this of Mine,
To love, to call, to wait, and see
　　You pass Me by, with never sign.

The thorns that pressed upon My brow,
　　No pain could give like this to Me;
The crown of rue you weave Me now,
　　You do not care if here I be.

Caroline Elizabeth MacGill.

TO HARSH JUDGMENT THINKING ITSELF WISDOM

So that was he whom you despise
Just passed before our casual eyes—
The broken wretch your scorn doth seek
As one scorn-worthy, being weak?
And was he weak, or was he strong
And gave he battle, hard and long?
Oh, looking so with alien stare
How may we judge and how declare
What massed files from nether Hell
He withstood before he fell?
What may we guess, what may we say
Of that sharp and deadly fray
When his soul in grievous fight
Closed with Evil in the night
Face to face and hand to hand
All in a strange and lonely land?

Oh, that fierce assault, the stark
And savage struggle in the dark,
When the lights of heaven grew cold
And the stormy darkness rolled
Over land and over sea
In a cloak of mystery.

Assault, repulse, assault again,
Oh, the never-easing strain,
Leaden moments of scant breath,
And the reeling ground beneath,
Till out-wearied with grim play
At last he faltered and gave way,
And while th' obscene and impious rout
Raised a wild, triumphant shout
There amid the loathly din
He fell before the hosts of sin.

Oh, looking now with alien eyes
What may we say and what surmise?
Of that grim battle, blow for blow,
What do we know, what do we know?

JOHN BUNKER.

TWO PERSONS

(Leaving Saint Vincent Ferrer's Church, New York)

"The stately nave, the gray light as of mist, the scent of incense, and
    the quiet air
Drew me from out my restless life,—facing the street, I shrink from
    leaving this, and that red spark hung there;
And yet between us, you the faithful one; I, in doubting reverence,
There rose a wall, impalpable and dense;—
Yes, we were separate!

"What came between us in the church? The noonday sun changing
  the dust of streets to diamond sand
Is not the same as when we entered. Has some unseen hand led
  you to cenacle, radiant with a light that's not of day?
You were so near; but suddenly your soul, forgetting me went far
  away,
While I could only try to read your heart—and wait.

"What, painting peace upon your face, has made you different
From last night on the balcony when silver gleamed upon the hills,
  and winds seemed spent
And weary with the scent of heliotrope,
And in the garden viols of our love spoke
And roses sang? but now you rise to heaven and—I remain below."

"That ruby light!" he said, impatient. "What mystery does it hide?
A symbol of the bleeding wound in your Lord's side?—
More like a little passion flower in bloom!
It seems to conquer love and life and me!" Still she stood, enwrapt.
  "Follow Our Lord into the upper room,"
She said, "sit with Saint John and Peter. You shall know."

MAURICE FRANCIS EGAN.

PROCESSIONAL

Twin candlesticks receive the light;
God's shrine with life again is bright;
An organ plays—a muted song
Unmuting starts a choir along,   ,
And swelling fills the church, the while
From vestry marching up the aisle
They come, youth first, its voice raised high,
Joy bringing, swinging, singing by;
Youth, adolescence, manhood, all
File slowly past me in my stall.
Sopranos, altos, pass along
Each filled with deeper throated song,

Each voice proclaiming in its way
Life's subtle slow advancing day.
The tenors, after them the bass,
More slowly modulate their pace,
And pour with vibrant strength and power
Their very souls into the hour.
God's minister, his face ashine
With Heaven's glory ends the line.
They've past. Still mingled melody
Fills nave, apse, all with harmony
Till, chancel reached, their voices die.
So life, from birth to death, files by.
But hold! Service has just begun!
Life begins when life is done.

ROGER L. WARING.

THE TWO SERMONS

The preacher spoke of pride and lust; his voice droned like a bee;
The gold light on a blood-red pane woke wordless thoughts in me.
He spoke of love in a half-dream, but in the altar shade,
The nodding of a candle-flame a winged love had made.
He spoke of showered loveliness his wrinkled heart knew not;
The incense like a pale blue mist a fairer beauty taught.
He spoke of hope, and yet I heard but dimly what he said;
I saw a tiny lamp and flame of lowly burning red.
He spoke of God, and God's great might, but all my soul could see
Were towering arches, height on height, in calm sublimity.
He spoke of death, but in my soul there was no thought of death;
I saw a white archangel poised athwart a window's breath.
He spoke dim words of Golgotha, and Christ upon a rood;
I saw a jeweled chalice hide in gold its cup of Blood.
He spoke of hell and Paradise, and yet I had not heard;
My chained soul had visioned the Unutterable Word.

MYLES CONNOLLY.

ETERNALS

There will be dreams when steel and stone
    Have won their last assault;
When towered cities' dust is blown
    Into an unsealed vault.

There will be dreams when mountains fall
    Into the burning earth,
When darkness flowing over all
    Will frustrate time's rebirth.

There will be dreams when all that man
    Achieves with nimble thought,
Has decomposed and nothing can
    From chaos then be caught.

There will be dreams, however we
    May term their last release
From doubting hope to verity
    Of everlasting peace.

CATHERINE M. BRESNAN.

THE VISION IMMORTAL

Not life alone—but we ourselves—
    The vision that we bring
Unto its reading—this it is
    That makes us slave or king.

Who walks in golden comradeship
    Of Faith-illumined thought,
For him each day new miracles
    Of beauty shall be wrought.

Of beauty filling to the brim
    The chalice of his need,
And aureoling with its rays
    Each dream and word and deed.

And bright upon his eyes shall shine
    The lyric light that falls
From wonder's eyes and on his ears
    Shall sound her sunrise calls.

For beauty's source and fount is his—
    The Vision uncreate—
That fuses his mortality
    With God's immortal state.

ELEANOR ROGERS COX.

INSCRIPTION FOR A BOOK

Of old so precious was a book that key
    And lock were put upon it, to withhold
    Its treasured lettering against the mold
And dull erasure of the years . . . But see
How artfully the pen, how lovingly
    The prayerful brush, their age-old lore unfold,
    How rich in azure tracery enscrolled
The poet's dream, a golden filigree!

. . . Dust is the golden brush; the artful hand
    Is vanished as the insubstantial air;
        The book lies open now; its azures pale
Before the noonbright day. What can withstand
    Time's blurring light? The dream, the vision, the prayer:
        These only through the ages shall prevail.

Look on this new-made page, and, overwise,
    As is the wont of us in human way,
        Smile as you've often smiled an idle day
To see the labored script that faded lies
Writ on an ancient vellum . . . Yes, but sighs
    Shadow your smiling now; these thoughts that play
    Freshly across this glistening sheet array
More than the living present for your eyes.

. . . The past is here already! Turn the page—
Or here or there, mark you how swift the time
   Runs from the moment to the hour. The past
Is here already! Youth, and sudden . . . age!
   Turn back! Turn back! I write my little rhyme
   To catch your heart before the lock is fast.

Charles Phillips.

BEFORE ETERNITY

Day after day, and the moldy mill stones turn,
Grinding out time in a dusty iron urn;
Day after day, and the dawns their splendor shed,
And one more day is numbered with the dead:
Day after day, and the west with red is flushed,
And a weary world in slumbrous dreams is hushed.
Day follows day and still the dull wheels grind,
Sad days and glad days are sternly left behind.
Yes, time runs its mill, turning without rest,
With never a lull to heed the least behest.

Grind, grind, grind with never tiring might,
And fair golden locks are ground to powdered white.
Grind, grind, grind and the cheerful ruddy face
Shows through its furrows where time has left its trace.
Bright eyes grow dull and a merry voice is still,
And a life has been ground in hoary time's grist mill.

J. R. N. Maxwell, S.J.

TIME

Time, calendars, hours, clocks
Are incorporeal rusty locks,
Restraining men of swaddled minds
In prisons of assorted kinds.

If one has spirit-kindled strength
He learns to break the locks at length,
And walks abroad at liberty,
Breathing a fresh eternity.

One brooding hour on moor or beach,
With gulls and haunting sea, may reach
Beyond the life of graveyard stones
That crumple over crumbling bones.

Smart lackeys of the punctual sun
May eat and barter on the run;
But one should pause, who thinks or prays.
For days are eons, eons days!

EARL BIGELOW BROWN.

THE MASTER BUILDER SPEAKS

I tell you sand will not support the shock!
Dig farther—dig till you strike the living rock!
That's my advice—my last word. I'll not stand
The consequence of building on this sand.
I've seen them fall, go crashing one by one,
These lordly towers, from here to Babylon.
(They smile! My God! the smile that Babel saw!)

Well then! Cast up that steel of Roman law
Stark to the morning sun, for in it thrill
The souls of Caesars dead, imperial still,
Who rule us from the tomb. Now flesh it o'er
With more than Parian marble—more, far more!
With visible soul, the glory that was Greece,
Aching through Athens still and will not cease—
Hellenic loveliness, Promethean pain,
Icarian thought, too daring to attain.
Thus boned and bodied, let your towers rise;
Steel-sired, mist-mothered, let them front the skies.

Now clothe it with the glowing dream that once
Stole over sleeping Europe—Renaissance
'Tis now miscalled,—'twas dream, sheer, golden dream
Begot of dawn, and in the day's full beam
We could not hold the fire and air of it.
Now let the lightning of the Gallic wit
Play through the frankincense of Gaelic soul
And let the Anglo-Saxon organ roll
Of the mastery and the mystery of the sea.

Complete, you say?   Shall stand while time shall be?
Magnificent?   Yes—and yet—that sound!   Stand clear!
Back quickly!   Back!   God! how that tower falls sheer!
That sand gave way.   Sand never has sufficed.
Will you build now upon the Rock that's Christ?

LOUIS F. DOYLE, S.J.

HOMAGES

THE CARPENTER

He was the man of action,
  Captain of industry,
And his soul was like a single pearl
  Lost in the sea.

He was up and doing
  By daylight and by dark,
And the sheltered veins within him
  Sang like a lark.

He swung the adze, the hammer,
  He paid the public tax,
And his heart burned like a candle
  Virginal, of wax.

Coming home at evening
  He had his loaf and wine,
And he saw in a young Child's eyes
  All the stars shine.

He read in a Woman's face
  The sum of love and beauty,
As all the while he went about
  Doing his duty.

Daily his carpenter's shop
  Was swept by seraphim,
Almost, the Son of God
  Was lackey to him.

An eagle once on Patmos
  Soaring, saw and heard
The secret things that Joseph knew
  Who never said a word.

Most blessed, baffling man,
  History's one sphinx,—
It must be heaven is
  What Joseph thinks.

CHARLES L. O'DONNELL, C.S.C.

THE CROWN

She had twelve stars for diadem,
  She had for footstool the full moon,
Her quiet eyes out-shining them
  Kept memories of the night and noon
And the still morns at Nazareth
When in her arms the Child drew breath.

So safe, so warm, he slept by her
  In her enfolding arms at peace,
Her milky Babe, little and dear;
  And yet the tree that should be His
Grew in the forest, wide and high,
Whose branches should fill all the sky.

He made twelve stars into her crown
  And set the moon beyond her feet;
He was King in Jerusalem town
  With twelve spines for His coronet
To pierce the brain, the blood and bone
That thought of man's Redemption.

Oh, when she answered Gabriel
  With "Be it done!" could she foresee
The high pangs, that she took as well
  With Bethlehem, should be Calvary,

Or was that name of high bliss
Born with sharp pains, fierce agonies?

Hath she beneath her crown of stars
    Remembrance of the thorns wherewith
Her people crowned her Son? What scars
    Redder than roses in a wreath
Doth she wear in a coronal
Under the lights that rise and fall?

                        KATHARINE TYNAN.

A GIFT OF FLOWERS

A basket of roses for the Royal House of David,
    A harvest of blossoms in the spring;
Chrysanthemums and daisies for the ladies of Jerusalem
    And lilies for the daughters of the king.

Lilies out in Galilee, opening in April;
    Sunflowers to pluck and carry home;
Poppies for high priestesses and myriads of tulips
    For the wives of the emperors of Rome.

But ah, come and wander, meek Maid of Nazareth,
    Wander by the brook and by the lea;
A sweet, little, meek, frail, lonely-by-the-wayside,
    Shadow-blue violet for thee.

                        LEONARD FEENEY, S.J.

QUESTIONNAIRE

What did you think of, Mary,
    As He looked up from your breast?
I saw His eyes like stars
    In the early evening west.

And when you bathed His limbs
    In waters warm and sweet?
I loved Him, adorable, perfect
    From head to perfect feet.

What waking vision stirred you
    As He slept, small and weak?
For hours and hours I watched
    The little curve of His cheek.

And when the first words came
    At length from His learning lips?
I could feel my blood listening
    Down to my finger-tips.

On that amazing day
    Along the temple hall
He taught the Scribes, you thought?—
    My Boy grows straight and tall.

At Cana when your words
    Hurried His coming hour,
You saw?—I saw His hands,
    Beautiful, with power.

Oh, and when at the last
    He was slain by the crowd?
Never of my dear Son
    Was I so fond, so proud.

Then, when His cheek to yours
    Lay lifeless and cold?
I thought how never now
    Would my Son grow old.

But, ah, on Easter morn
    You had your heart's desire!

He came to me at dawn
And helped me with the fire.

Did you know that He was God?
From Gabriel's word, of course,
Alpha, Omega, of all
The End and the Source.

But, women of all the world
That ever children bore,
Remember, He is my Son,
And human, forevermore.

CHARLES L. O'DONNELL, C.S.C.

PRESENTATION OF THE VIRGIN

They parted from their little maid—
So glad and shy, and unafraid
With strangeness so she were with God.
Exalted, humbly proud, they trod
The Temple's courts and stairs, again
The City crossed, came home . . . and then—
Her dove sat brooding; garden nooks
Were empty of her and the brook's
Loud chattering seemed strangely stilled today . . .
There was a place she used to play
Beneath the fig tree—secret games
With twigs and speckled stones in frames
Of shavings; hollows in the ground
She filled with petals while the sound
Of little tunes she made came soft
To Joachim, who worked aloft
The arbor on his vines.   Here stayed
He silent. . . . Anna, while she laid
Aside her mantle, bent her head—
Looking long upon a child's low bed.

FLORENCE CHAMPREUX MAGEE.

DIALOGUE

"Good morning, sir," said Joachim.
"Good morning, sir," said I to him;
"And how does little Mary be?"
"The queen of little girls," said he.

"She's off to sleep at candle-light
  And never bothers us at night;
Always as happy as a rose—
  She'll be a wonder when she grows."

"Well, little marvel people can
  That such a child should come to Anne."
"It's true for you," said Joachim,
  And then, "Good day," said I to him.

THOMAS BUTLER FEENEY, S.J.

MATER LUCIS AUREAE

*"Then seyde the meydon full myldely,
  He schall be dere welcum to me."*

The maid Saint Mary drifts afield,
  God-touched, withouten wem,
And singing she culls beside a weald
  Pale stars-o'-Bethlehem.

While she passes along the vineyard walls
  In the dewy sunrise hour,
The swallow's far faint twitter falls
  Through the almond trees in flower.

The fragrant winds by Nazareth town
  Make the poppies fade and flare,
And toss the almond petals down
  On the waves of her spun bronze hair.

The merle bells here, the lark hymns there,
    Before the throne of God;
And Gabriel stoops through the sapphire air
    To kiss where her feet have trod.

Astonied she sees his love-rapt face,—
    Her meek assent is heard,
And into the shoreless sea of her grace
    Sinks the priceless pearl of the Word.

                                AUSTIN O'MALLEY.

MATERNITY

Since that Word of Wisdom was
Announced by Gabriel, and because
He rested in thy womb a while
Of Spirit-shadowed days, we style
        Thee Mother of God.

Because thy hallowed flesh was one
With Emmanuel, Jehovah's Son,
When Love inspired the singing flame
Of thy canticle, all peoples name
        Thee Mother of God.

Since that thou wert the maiden who,
Still virgin as the angels knew
Came vested in a boding veil
To Bethlehem, all nations hail
        Thee Mother of God.

Because, while night was big with earth
And heaven with star, thy flesh gave birth
To Jesus Christ within a stall;
Our little ones, thy children, call
        Thee Mother of God.

Since that the Child Himself who was
Of thee, His creature yet thy Cause,
Did ever call thee mother, lo!
From Truth whose Word is Love we know
    Thee Mother of God,

Who yet would sing thy canticle.
Oh! may the Holy Spirit's will,
Being one with ours as with thine own,
O'ershadow soul and flesh and bone,
    Dear Mother of God.

So our Annunciation Day
Be made our soul's own Christmas; yea,
So that our Guardian speak the word
As Gabriel: "Hail, thou hast the Lord!"
    O Mother of God,

Thus to conceive our Christ! Ah, me
What mystic conceptivity:
At once both to conceive and give
Him birth who died that we might live!
    True Mother of God,

We ask thou intercede with prayer,
So that we may receive thy Care
In worthy bosoms, thou to whom
He came by way of virgin womb.
    Ah, Mother of God.

Do thou, as His hand-maiden, spin
That seamless robe of grace wherein
The Living Presence, vested thus,
Shall know thy care, as well as us
    Bemothering God!

Francis Carlin.

TO THE NURSE OF MAN

Shield me, O my nurse,
Be my protection against the danger-day;
From the eternal curse
Shield me, I pray.
Be my roof against the storm,
My buckler against His mighty wrath,
Save me from the devouring worm.
Look on my sin, and hide
It, not thy face.
Hear my plaint, kinswoman,
Full of grace.

Hear me, O my nurse,
Thou who wert nurse to the Heaven-King;
Show Him thy bosom fair,
Remind His drinking
Thy sweet milk, remind thy tears.
Thy stainlessness alone, thy ways
Alone can save me from foul sears
Of sin. Born for the weal
Of Adam's race,
Hear my creel, kinswoman,
Full of grace.

Lead me, O my nurse,
Through the wood safely, hold tight
My tugging hand in thine
In paths of right.
Thou who wert woodsman to tear
The roots of the gnarled tree of debt,
Thou who wert gardener to care
A new and golden tree,
Transcending space,
Hear my song, kinswoman,
Full of grace.

JAMES E. TOBIN.

TO A CARRARA VIRGIN

Madonna,
I have seen you come
Down the long stair
From heaven—
A crown of stars upon your hair,
Blue from the night in your eyes
And blue for your gown
Borrowed from summer skies.

Madonna,
I have seen you come
To the last stair leaning out
Until your hair
Like attar of roses
Through the orient dusk
Fell all along my arms outstretched.

Madonna,
Tonight
I am here,
But you are white;
You do not move.

SISTER MARIELLA, O.S.B.

STARS

Dear Lady, in the night's pale witching hour,
  When all God's starry garden is aglow
  With golden roses I have seen you go
From heaven's gate adown each jeweled bower,
Stooping to pluck a bud,—and now a flower.
  And when your arms were filled to overflow
  With treasures for your Lord, you smiled,—and so
Stole softly back into the King's high tower.

One night you dropped a rose; I saw it sweep
Down through the vasty reaches of the deep.
   It fell I know not where;—but if I knew,
      Across the world, love-pinioned, would I dart
Magi-like, to catch that rose from you
      And plant it in the garden of my heart.

JOHN F. QUINN, S.J.

THE FLAIL OF GOD

O Mother of God and Mistress of men,
Out of the heart of heaven when,
Oh, when will the fire-shod Angel fare
Forth through the still stars unaware,
And leap like a bolt through the distance down
Upon fleet, upon fosse, upon flaming town,
      And silence the guns on land and sea?

Wars there are and rumors of war;
   Nation and nation, king and king,
Battle anear, and battle afar,
   Half the world girt with a fiery ring.
In one place quake of the earth slew all.
Mammon and Moloch call and call.
      Famine there is and pest shall be.

Ah, well we know the end is not yet:
But, Mother of Pity, look thy fill
Where women work that men may kill,
And their eyes with blood are wet.
Children are reckoned to fill spent files.
The wounded lie in cathedral aisles.
      God and His people bivouac without.

Thousands are blown like shards into rain;
   Thousands slip down in the deep by night;

Thousands are mown like ripe, red grain;
　　Thousands are blasted and burnt in flight;
And the wounded lie, and die, and die,
A roaring hell is God's blue sky,
　　　And the sick are forgot in the rout.

Oh, ask of God to punish no more;
To stay His flail on the threshing-floor:
For millions are dead, and millions are maimed;
Sinned have we all, and our pride is tamed;
　　The people are weary, their princes are mad;
　　Even the child unborn is sad.
　　　　O Mother Mary, hear our plea!
　　　　Peace, oh, peace, let us have of thee!
　　　　　　　　　CHARLES MACKSEY, S.J.

AVE MARIA

The cold blue marble of your eyes seems warmer now
Than yesterday, Tall Lady, and your unmoving lips
Are eager now to speak; your immaculate brow
Is framed with candles slender as the fingertips
That hold the lilies shadowing your quiet breast
That seems almost to throb. . . . You are so near to me. . .
Your girded robes are moving on the scented crest
Of incense burning slowly to eternity,
And reaching vainly to the lofty awfulness
Above the clouds; above the stars and skies and all;
Beyond the walls of worldly love and loveliness;
Beyond unpillared heavens to the gold portal
Of sanctuary where you are.
　　　　　Here I may kneel
And talk to you, Fair Lady, while the unknowing winds
Are tearing at my heart.　Here I may know the feel
Of tenderness and love; the sainted ways and kinds
Of you, for I am flesh, though not stainless as you,
And Christ, your Son.

And if men are unanswering
And cannot find the fair white lilies that you strew
From heaven to earth, will you let me go gathering
Them up again to place them at your unflowered shrine?
And will you talk to me, Tall Lady, when the night
Comes slowly? Will you reach your lovely hands to mine
And lead me up the starlit ways of blue and white . . .
Over the faltered edges . . . up beyond the skies
To where you live, that I may know you smiling there
As I have seen a smile soften your marble eyes
And linger quietly like some forgotten prayer?

NORBERT ENGELS.

A BOUQUET OF STARS

If I could walk in the meadow of sky,
  With the sickle moon in my hand,
I'd cut all the blossoming point-petaled flowers,
  Till knee deep in stars I'd stand.

I'd gather them all in the gossamer veil
  That some call the Milky Way,
And carry them straight to a lovely maid:
  Our Lady, the Queen of May.

BERNARDINE BASSLER.

RENUNCIATION

O Virgin Mother of the Holy One,
Of what avail this strife 'twixt thee and me?
Lo, in this hour I give him back to thee:
Deal gently with thine erring human son.

I give him back, his spirit-wings release,
That he may rise beyond my yearning reach,
Beyond all sound of my impassioned speech,
And find, near thee, forgetfulness and peace.

Of alien creed, to thee I breathe one prayer:
Touch, if thou wilt, each letter of my name
That love has graven on his heart in flame,
And leave the imprint of thine image there.

Constance Davies-Woodrow.

FOLDING TIME
I
"Jesus, herds pursue
    Their scattered sheep;
'Tis time my Lambkin, too,
    Were safe in sleep."

"Mother, as you would;
    Upon your breast
I'll win Me bed and food,
    Yea, drink My rest."

II
"Mary, He's away!
    May one and all
Thus willingly obey
    Their slumber-call."

"Joseph, build a fold
    Of wattled gleams
And sheen o' thatch, to hold
    His fleecy dreams."

III
("Shepherds, gather nigh:
    Help Me pursue
Yon scattered lambkins, ay,
    And kidlings, too.")

"Waking, little Son?
    Lu-lay-na-shoon."
("But ninety-nine—there's one—")
    "Husheen-na-hoon."

Francis Carlin.

NOON IN NAZARETH

"Oh come, little Boy, it's time for rest,
  So heavy now, clouded Your eyes;
You woke with dawn, and noon's at the crest—
  I have heard Your soft-drawn sighs!

"But first, I must bathe these tired feet
  That have trudged with Your cart and sand
Past the door all morn . . . they're clean and sweet—
  So now, each dusty hand!

"See here is Your milk, so cool to quench
  Your thirst from the heat. I've made
Some small barley-loaves; we'll go to the bench
  And eat in the olive trees' shade. . ."

So still the noon! So soft bleat the kids!
  How faint from the hill come cries
Of children at play! He nods and His lids
  Come fluttering down, and rise

And fall; He is breathing deep and slow. . .
  On that brow what majesty grown!
Before Him, laid down, she kneels full low,
  Adoring God's Son and her own.
                              FLORENCE CHAMPREUX MAGEE.

THE PROPHECY

Without the Temple gates
  Sweet birds were chanting lyrics to the dawn,
And doves were cooing softly to their mates
  That long-remembered morn.

Within my arms enshrined
  Like snow-white flower with petals just unclosed
That lifts its face the new-born light to find,
  My little One reposed.

151

Ah, happy was my lot!
  All nature seemed the pathway to bedight
So wrapped was I in bliss, and I forgot
  The lonely cave at night.

When lo, from some far Hill
  A chill wind swept; the slumbering echoes woke,
And breath of doves and song of birds were still,
  And then—my glad heart broke!

"A sword thy soul shall tear."
  He gave Him back into my arms again,
My little Babe, that once was white and fair,
  Now bruised for sinful men.

I saw Him so once more—
  In death He rested on His Mother's knee,
And five deep wounds like roses red He bore,
  To pay the price of thee!

                              MABEL FARNUM.

THE LITTLE HOURS OF OUR LADY

I wonder what her thoughts had been,
Fair Heaven's Queen—
Not those great thoughts on which she pondered long,
But when, some early radiant morn,
She listened to a bird's God-praising song,
And watched her sturdy Son.

Or when, her task being done,
She gave to Him a little cake, and He
Drank from the jar she bore Him from the well,
(As she, within the Cenacle
Should one day sup with Him forever more).

152

The sun being high, she called Him from His play,
To quiet shelter by her distaff side,
And told Him stories of King David's day,
His ancient sire, while He
With sticks and stones rebuilt Adullam on the floor,
And laughed in mimic pride to see
His skill, calling to Joseph at the door.
The while "King David" poured the sacrificial drink
Did her thoughts dare the brink
Of prophecy and angel memory?

Midday. The Sun majestically gives
His glory unto God by whom all nature lives.
The Child is sleeping, and His mother weaves
The coat that He shall wear
Unto Jerusalem. Upon it falls a tear
As every mother's heart in sorrow grieves—
Beholding years to come
When all her love can save Him from no pain,
No pang of anguish fend Him by her care,
But by a hooting mob shall see Him slain.

The shadows lengthen. At His little task
Merrily He brings the workshop chips,
And piles them on the hearth, running to ask
If all is well. "We'll drive away the dark
When Father comes." Oh did her heart
Shudder at those awful clouds which once should part
And show to her His blanched and silent lips?

But now He leaps and sings, for down the road
Comes Joseph. The Lad will share the load,
And running takes the workman's tools,
Joyously He brings them all within,
And fetches wine at her request.
(So too at her behest
He lifts our burdens, and our hot sorrow cools,

153

Bidding us be merry, for the light
He hath prepared for us at eventide).

And then the crown of all her day,
Ceasing His play
Wearily He slips within her arms,
Safe from all alarms,
His perfect need of her she can fulfill,
Oh wonder of God's will!
Oh sweet and still and silent hour,
Height of Love's power!
Again her Son—and God—upon her breast,
Taking His rest.
Oh blessed among women, and blest womb
That gave Him room,
When He would come from heaven high
For man to live, and die,
Did not man's flesh deny.
Ah listen, while a lullaby she sings
To seraph harping strings
"My soul, rejoicing in my Saviour high,
The Lord doth magnify."

CAROLINE ELIZABETH MACGILL.

THE BLIND MAN OF JERICHO

In your dungeon blindness it is always night,
　　No bird of dawning sings to you of day.
　　You hear but see not children in their play;
Feel the noon warm, but never see noon bright.
And then He comes mid salvos left and right
　　Of all the town folk lining up the way.
　　And high above their shouts He hears you pray,
"O Lord that I may see," and gives you sight.

Now spread before you is the noon warm sky,
　　And ancient fields where gleaned the heartsick Ruth,

And tropic sand dust whitening all the plain.
But what are these? He in His passing by
Floods the dark prison of your soul with truth;
What care you if your eyes fall blind again!

PATRICK J. CARROLL, C.S.C.

SILHOUETTES

I

Bethlehem asleep
And far away
The Magi. . . .
Cardboard images
Against a purple wall.

II

Torches glinting
On their swords and shields. . .
On faces hard as both;
And one who leers
Across the shadows,
"Which is He?"

III

The cross!
A bloody sun,
And shadows racing earthward.
Far below,
The Jews, like frightened children,
Huddled in the dark.

IV

Three crosses on a skull-shaped hill,
And at the foot of one. . . .
A woman . . . weeping.

C. T. LANHAM.

COMPASSION

Soft were her arms and young where He lay curled,
  She was not very old the day He died,
  But when the spear withdrew that pierced His side,
No one was quite so old in all the world.

I would make a song as evening hushed and dim,
  O Lady, for the tears that you have shed,
  Could you forget one hour that He is dead
And to your breast, a Baby, gather Him.

CHARLES L. O'DONNELL, C.S.C.

LAMENT FOR A POOR POET

He sits at the foot of Golgotha,
  And out of his singing soul
He fashions songs to make His Lord
  A shining aureole.

But all the songs he sings are vain,
  And all his singing dross—
For he sits at the foot of Golgotha
  While Christ hangs on the cross.

And yet His Lord may deem his songs
  Were better sung than not,
For they, at least, remembered Him
  When other songs forgot.

MYLES CONNOLLY.

NONE SO BLIND

Had I gone down to Galilee
  Upon a certain day,
Had I walked through the market place
  Thronged as a shoaling sea,
I might have passed a Certain Face
  In my oblivious way;

Or had I glimpsed a cresset brow,
  A white light lifting high—
No brazen crown nor raiment—
  (As dull then, heart, as now?)
Or would my arrogance have bent,
  Or passed in blindness by . . .

POWER DALTON.

"AND WOMEN MUST WEEP"

(A woman's song of comfort)

There was no sadness anywhere,
  No laughter and no song,
As we sat there in pain and dearth
  And brooded on our wrong.
There was no light in all the sky,
  No light on earth or sea,
As I wept there with Mary
  And Mary wept with me.

Pale Mary said no word to me
  As in my arms she wept.
Above us gloomed the bloody tree,
  While Pilate's conscience slept.
Light seemed to creep like carrion blood
  On man's contumacy,
As I wept there with Mary
  And Mary wept with me!

There was no sadness anywhere,
  No longer could I weep.
The planets quiring in her hair
  Lulled all my doubts to sleep.
I wore my crown of womanhood,
  Sweet Christ: my soul leapt free,
As I clung to Queen Mary
  And Queen Mary clung to me!

R. R. MACGREGOR.

CONSEQUENCES

It is important that You came and died;
  You might have paid our debt in Nazareth
And gone away, and rested satisfied
  To leave us our monopoly of death.

How should we lift a cradle up on high,
  What cloud of heaven point to as Your bed?
We who can show this hill, against this sky,
  Where You were hanged, and all men saw You, dead.

Your cross commands the cross-roads of the world,
  Your death makes death a door that was a prison,
And, crowning wonder over all unfurled,
  Except You died, how could You be arisen?

Except You died, while horror smote the sun,
  You had not said, of all Your words, this word—
"Father, forgive them!"—Lucifer, undone,
  Well might have wept, as lost in hell he heard.

CHARLES L. O'DONNELL, C.S.C.

ADDRESS TO THE CROWN

He made them and He called them good
As they had grown in the bramble wood,
Long and glistening, green and brown
Thorns that now in a woven crown
Approached to clasp His stricken Head,
As gently chiding them He said:
"Children, My Thorns, on the wild thorn tree
That were your proper place to be.
Along your woods young April goes
And sweet in the brake is the wind that blows.
Here indeed you have lost your skies;
Why are you twisted circle-wise,
What do you here in the hands of men?"

And it seems the Thorns gave answer then;
"You know, my Lord, it is not we
Have left our place on the bramble tree,
But evil hearts that cry for Blood
Have torn us away from the April wood.
There is a thing which men call sin,
We think it is this that drives us in:
With Blood above, and Blood below,
You know we would not have it so,
With Blood below, and Blood above,
Believe it is a clasp of love
We take upon Your holy Head,
Forgive us living, and love us, dead."

And He who had made them and called them good,
The long sharp thorns of the young spring wood,
He bowed His holy Head to them
And went to His death in their diadem.

CHARLES L. O'DONNELL, C.S.C.

THE PRAYER OF A THIEF

An outcast from whose touch my brothers fly,
 Yet one with Him whose spirit I profaned,
I climbed the tree of death, and 'neath the sky
 Of Calvary, I stole the Heart I pained.

It was not prophet of the Olden Law,
 Nor king arrayed in purple majesty,
Nor John the Baptist whom the angels saw,
 Nor Thy sweet Mother entering with Thee.

But hand in hand, 'fore heaven's wondering eyes,
A thief went in with Thee to Paradise.

JOHN B. KELLY.

VIA DOLOROSA

Out the Damascus Gate it ran,
    A weary, cheerless road
Along which stumbled once a Man,
    A cross-tree for his load.
The street was teeming with the throng,
    The air was chill and gray,
The hour when Jesus passed along
    That Dolorosa Way.

It wound a slope that flung its height
    Against a sullen sky.
Upon a summit—tragic sight—
    Three crosses lifted high.
But lo, beyond them, manifold
    The lifting glow of day.
It ended at the gates of gold,
    That Dolorosa Way.

CLARENCE E. FLYNN.

"O FELIX CULPA!"

Then gazed the wild wood dumb with awe,
    Staring with eyeballs opened wide,
At one grown conscious of a law
    And lifted suddenly to pride.

The apex of creation in
    His shame, creation, envious sees—
Magnificently robed with sin,
    Knowing the roots of mysteries.

Hot-footed hurrying through the immense
    The winds their happy tidings tell,
That man, exchanging innocence—
    And gladly! for the fires of hell,

Proves his long-boasted power to choose,
    To leave the good and take the ill;
Free, with his soul to save or lose,
    By warrant of its royal will.

But hidden from the awestruck eyes,
    Which see the sentenced rebels go,
Are those tall towers of Paradise
    Where strange exultant rumors blow;

Where seated at the council board
    The Three-in-One debate Their plan,
The Incarnation of the Word,
    The sorrows of the Son of Man.

THEODORE MAYNARD.

EASTERTIDE

All you that weep, all you that mourn,
    All you that grieving go,
Lift up your eyes, your heads adorn,
    Put off your weeds of woe.
The sorrows of the Passion week
    Like tearful dreams are fled,
For He hath triumphed whom you seek,
    Is risen, that was dead.

Oh you who to the sepulcher
    At break of morning bring
The tribute of your spice and myrrh
    To balm our murdered King,
Each cleft of His forsaken tomb
    With Easter sun is red,
For He you straightened mid the gloom
    Is risen, that was dead.

See, all about the prostrate stone
    Its abject sentries stand,
Death, with its diadem downthrown,
    And fear with fettered hand,
Lo! captive of the nails and spear
    Captivity is led,
For Love that conquers death and fear
    Is risen, that was dead.

HENRY LONGAN STUART.

EASTER

Gray in the east, that slowly turns to gold,
Shadows that pass, and as they pass unfold.

All that the earth had stored of leaf and flower,
Bourgeoning forth, triumphant in this hour.

Gray, the hollowed rock wherein He sleeps;
Grief in the heart of one Mary as she weeps.

Golden the light that bursts, dispelling gloom;
Radiant the Flower of Men, rising from the tomb.

CAROL STONE.

ALLELUIAH

Now earth's adoring trees,
Gold-leaving, play their vernal symphonies
For Him,
In unison with flame-bright seraphim.
All birds that post by land or sea or river—
Vast tribes of the finny deep—
Where citadels of silence downward sweep—
Make festival of gladness for the Giver
Of myriad forms of life His hands hold dear—
Now soars the high hosanna-hymn of cheer—
Out of the heart of man and beast goes fear,
Abjectly beaten; tier on tier of motion,

Ringed by the rhythmic wings of moon and ocean,
Is charged with electric waves of heavenly joy—
Humanity, new-born, like a laughing boy,
Leaps up to fling its morning-song to the winds—
Crushed now are sin's black blinds!
The imperial Sun,
As royal governor of the plains and hills,
Elysian light through sleeping darkness spills.
Rose-blankets, thick with fragrance lush and warm,
Where late were cold and storm,
The south wind lays in peace along the world.
'Twixt heaven and earth Christ's flag of love, unfurled,
Unites the hearts of men,
To make of them a garden green again.

Ay, glorious all the eyes that strained in sorrow,
Glorious every face that feared the morrow,
Glorious all the lands that swam in war—
Look ye, the Burning Breast we waited for!
The powerful Hand uplifted, not for smiting,
But for an infinite righting
Of ills that seared the bending backs of peoples—
From spires and domes and music-haunted steeples,
Let wingéd joy go forth, to mount like fire,
In mammoth blending with th' angelic choir.

J. CORSON MILLER.

CORAM SANCTISSIMO

Beautiful, O Love, Thou art,
Print Thine image on my heart!
Fairer than the rising sun,
Fairer than the dawn begun,
Fairer than the morning star,
Fairer, my Beloved, far
Than all earthly loveliness
Is Thy mystical caress!

Beautiful, O Love, Thy face,
Beautiful, this quiet place
Where Thy glory dwells content
In the Blessed Sacrament.
Beautiful this mystery
Of a God's humility,
Beautiful Thy smile above
Weary millions seeking Love.

MARY DIXON THAYER.

THE HARVEST BENEDICTION

"Whisper!" the cockle said
To the tare: "The vine's blood, shed
On yonder cross-shaped bars,
Is now but wine in jars."

"Aye, true!" the tare replied:
"And the wheat's flesh, having died
On a scythe-shaped cross, but rose
As bread yon sheaves inclose."

'Twas harvest-time. On high
The wild geese mowed the sky;
While breezes, in the wake
Of the reapers, came to rake
Both drift and windrow bright
As the yellow sheaves o' light,
That stood a-field and leaned
O'er dusk where shadows gleaned.

Along the splendor's edge,
The gray horizon-hedge
Was streaked with sheen, like haws
That sparrows deck with straws;
While martins cut a swath
In the daylight's aftermath
Of gloaming-gold that lay
Like buttercups in hay.

And so it came to pass
That a lark, from after-grass,
Sang up to silence where
The hush put on his prayer;
While passing swallows signed
Air-crosses on the wind
'Gainst eery bats that glide
On winds at witching-tide.

The clouds, from out their blue
Deep font of holy dew,
Then sprinkled kneeling sheaves
And bowing vineyard-leaves;
As the aged sun, who wore
God's vestment-gold, went o'er
The hidden yield to bless
Christ's Own Concealedness.

Then slowly from the East
Cowled twilight came, as priest
In cope o' silver-sheen,
Behind a hedge rood-screen.
And while the hills were hazed
With a smokiness, he raised
The monstrance of the night
Whose moon was wafer-white.

O'er vesperal incense
He raised Beneficence:
The moon as Host: the one
He held, in benison,
Until the quiet glow
Blest wine and bread, and so
Both Bread and Wine but for
The secret Harvester.

Then stars, their Lord's elect,
Stood up to genuflect

At the exposition of
Their Sacrament of Love:
And when it lay at last
In a tabernacle vast
As the evening's dark, 'twas then
The corn-crakes sang "Amen."

"Whisper!" said the vine
To the wheat: "This blood of mine,
That was but lately freed
Will yet be Blood indeed!"

"Aye, true!" the wheat replied:
"And this flesh of mine, that died
A-field, will yet arise
As Flesh of sacrifice!"

FRANCIS CARLIN.

A FIELD OF WHEAT

'Tis midnight and the prairie owl is lazy by the lake,
  And half of him is sleeping, for half of him is sly.
But one side of his ugly face is very wide-awake
  With the moonbeams of midnight in his eye.

'Tis starlight and the prairie owl is watching the tall sheaves,
  Those tireless, ever-twisting, swishy silences of grain,
All tangled and wind-laced and fluttering their leaves
  And murmuring and moaning in their pain.

"Some of us," they whisper, "shall ripen in the spring
  And feed the hungry multitudes beyond the land and sea,
And some of us shall tremble on the table of the King.
  Ah which of us, dear brothers, shall it be?

"And which of us shall falter when the wagon load is high,
  And fall from the heavy harvest when the men are hauling in,
And trampled in the darkness of the furrows shall we lie
  And dream forevermore what might have been!

"O Sacred Bread, O mystic Host, O snowy Gown of God!
    O dream of every blade of wheat that flickers in the sun—
And shall we rise up beautiful and fragrant from the sod
    And be the raiment for the Holy One!"

'Tis starlight and the prairie owl has let his eyelid close,
    For tired heads must droop at last and birds may slumber sweet;
But the waves rise, and the waves fall, and only the wild wind knows
    The everlasting restlessness of wheat.

LEONARD FEENEY, S.J.

EUCHARIST

I will have this Sacrament—
Eucharist of raying light,
Particle on particle,
One to all and all to one,
Hidden flower or skyey pine,
All to one and one to all;
Even so, the blade, the weed,
Feeding on the Entire Sun,
One to all and all to one.

I will have this Sacrament. . .
One to all and all to one.

CHARLES PHILLIPS.

SALUTE TO THE LAMB OF GOD

We will go softly, softly—
In moccasins of peace we will go—
As soft as the fingers of twilight stroke young trees
When no winds blow.
Away with the harsh harangue of the horns of glory!
Away with the strident music of place and power!
Salute the Lamb of God,
This is *His* hour!

Too much we have memorialized the story
Of the sowers of blood and of fire—the swingers of guns,
The delugers of death, where the great sea-monster runs—
We will go softly, softly,
Bearing banners of praise and of prayer,
Revering the Author of a plan of life more fair
Than all the man-made sophistries of time.
Wherefore, my song, be soft; like incense, rhyme
Ascend in humble homage to the Lord—
The Second One of the Trinity—adored
Unceasingly by hosts angelical.
Yet we are *men*: our tongues antiphonal
Shall not forget the Sacrifice He made—
The Life laid down—the evening that He prayed
For strength, and all the bitter cup was pressed
Against His bleeding Breast.
Too long, too long
The world bows down to the gods of greed and wrong!
Today we come, bearing a simple song
Spun out of silence; we would weave Him our years
In penitential wreaths; a tribute of tears
We would pay Him for love's high sacrament
He left us as a lasting monument—
The red-rose fire of His dear, untiring love.
"This is My Body," He said,
"This is My Blood that is shed
For the salvation of men,"
And then
In that half-darkened, blessed banquet-hall,
The Master gave Communion at evenfall.

Let all the trees, the flowers, the mountains and the seas,
The winds and the rains, the sky's golden galaxies,
The suns rising and setting, the beasts of the wild,
The mother in mirth and in sorrow, the rollicking child,
The fruits and the harvests of meadow, garden and field,
The energy oozing from seeds new vigor to yield—

Let all these vigil today, and with one great voice,
Entwined with the voices of men, rejoice, rejoice—
But softly, softly, as once on Tabor's peak
The Vision flamed, and the eyes of men grew meek.
Softly, softly, not as an eagle cries,
But soft as the hush when a lamb in suffering dies,
We will go singing, singing with one accord
The love of the Eternal Lover—
The Christ—*Our Lord!*

J. CORSON MILLER.

INDEX OF AUTHORS

176